ASTROLOGY 101

FROM **SUN SIGNS** TO **MOON SIGNS**, YOUR GUIDE TO **ASTROLOGY**

101

KATHLEEN SEARS

Adams Media

New York London Toronto Sydney New Delhi

Adams Media
An Imprint of Simon & Schuster, Inc.
57 Littlefield Street
Avon, Massachusetts 02322

For information about special discounts for bulk purchases, please contact Simon & Schuster Special Sales at 1-866-506-1949 or business@simonandschuster.com.

The Simon & Schuster Speakers Bureau can bring authors to your live event. For more information or to book an event contact the Simon & Schuster Speakers Bureau at 1-866-248-3049 or visit our website at www.simonspeakers.com.

Interior images © iStockphoto.com

Manufactured in the United States of America

10 9 8 7 6

Library of Congress Cataloging-in-Publication Data has been applied for.

ISBN 978-1-4405-9473-1
ISBN 978-1-4405-9474-8 (ebook)

CONTENTS

INTRODUCTION

Dating back to the ancient Egyptians, astrology has been a source of prophecy and lore for thousands of years. This venerable system is based on the idea that the positions of the stars, planets, and other heavenly bodies have a profound impact on events here on Earth. The month and day of your birth is linked inextricably to the movements of worlds millions of miles away.

In ages past, astrologers were widely consulted for their readings of the zodiac. In the Middle Ages, kings and emperors employed court astrologers, whose charge it was to cast horoscopes for their royal patrons. During the Renaissance, astrologers continued to flourish even as much astrological lore was incorporated into the new science of astronomy. But even today, tens of thousands of people believe in astrology and follow with interest their horoscopes in the newspapers and online.

In this book you'll find both the history and lore of astrology. You'll learn the signs of the planets and how to interpret them. You'll hear about famous astrologers and their predictions for the future—from the ancient Roman writer Ptolemy to Elizabeth I's court magician John Dee. You'll see the profound cultural impact of astrology, in literature, art, and music. You'll follow its long, slow decline in the face of modern science and its revival as an important part of the New Age movement today. And you'll learn the practical aspects of astrology: how to read a birth chart, how to cast a horoscope, and how to find what the stars say about your future in love, in money, and much more.

So prepare for a breathtaking journey that encompasses the past, present, and future. Let's begin *Astrology 101*.

CHAPTER 1

THE STORY OF ASTROLOGY

From the time we learned to walk upright, humans looked at the heavens above them and wondered.

What were the bright points of light that shone in the night sky? Were they fires burning far away in the vast darkness? Were they gods? Were they something else unknown?

In today's well-lit, urban-based world, it's hard to realize just what the night sky looked like to our ancestors. Today, when we look up in the darkness, we see a few stars and planets. If we live in rural areas we can see more. Perhaps, with the aid of a simple telescope, we can make out the dim luminosity of the Milky Way and a few of the most distant planets such as Jupiter and Saturn. But imagine living in a world almost without light at night, where the only source of illumination came from a few campfires. The cosmos, filled with starlight, must have seemed a mighty wonder, beyond the grasp of humans, solid and immovable as the earth beneath them.

And yet . . . as these people watched, they realized that the stars were *not* immovable. They rose and fell in a rhythm that could be tracked and predicted. At certain times and in certain seasons the same groups of stars appeared in the same place. Among this fixity, though, some stars appeared to move in a different fashion. The ancient Greeks, more than three thousand years ago, called them *planetes,* or "wandering stars."

These were the planets, of which the ancients knew only those that could be seen with the naked eye: Mercury, Venus, Mars, Jupiter, and Saturn.

As the centuries came and went, people charted the movement of these planets. They believed that celestial cycles could only be the work of gods, and since the gods controlled the fate of men and women it was only natural to believe that the planets and stars influenced human affairs as well. The planets were given the names of gods. The Romans called the red planet Mars, the god of war. The brightest star in the sky they named Venus, for the goddess of love (a serious misnomer, it turns out, since Venus, as shown by modern observation and space probes, is a thoroughly nasty place).

This evolution of human understanding of the skies forms the cradle of astrology, a theory that stretches from the ancient world down to our own day.

ASTROLOGY'S BEGINNINGS

From Babylon to Ancient Greece

The birth of astrology depended on three things: imagination, observation, and mathematics. The first two were common enough in the ancient world. The third developed gradually.

About 2000 B.C.E. in the city-state of Babylon in Mesopotamia, priests were becoming adept at reading the future in a variety of ways: through watching the flight of birds, in the entrails of sacrificed animals, and in the movement of the stars and other heavenly bodies. By the seventeenth century B.C.E., they had compiled elaborate tables charting these movements—the first astrological documents of which we know.

The Venus Tablet

The Venus Tablet of Ammisaduqa refers to a tablet recording observations about the movement of the planet Venus. It was written in cuneiform, the writing style of early Mesopotamia, and was probably compiled around the seventeenth century B.C.E. It was evidently a document of some importance, since a number of copies of it still exist (albeit often in fragmentary form). The object of observing Venus was evidently to make predictions about the reign of various kings, including Ammisaduqa, for whom the tablet is named.

During the next thousand years, astrological predictions continued to be refined, and by the eighth century B.C.E., the libraries in Babylon contained more than 7,000 astrological portents that priests could consult. These were known as the *Enuma Anu Enlil*. The Babylonians had a considerable advantage over other contemporary civilizations in compiling this material because their understanding of mathematics was the most advanced in the ancient world. By 500 B.C.E. they had invented the zodiac.

The Hermetic Tradition

Babylonian zodiacal lore made its way to Egypt where it mixed and assimilated Egyptian mystical and religious traditions. By the sixth and seventh centuries B.C.E., these had also become intermingled with Greek beliefs. Among the most important products of this mixing was the creation of what became known as the Hermetic tradition. The Greek god Hermes, the messenger of the gods, also had features of a number of other gods, including the Egyptian god Thoth. Through a process that is not very clear, he became known as *trismegistos,* which means that three adjectives, some of which were associated with Thoth, were applied to him. Finally he was called Hermes Trismegistus, which we might translate as Hermes the Thrice-Renowned. A large body of writings grew up in association with him, known as *Hermetic* writings. These included a number of important astrological documents that incorporated and integrated Greek, Babylonian, and Egyptian astrological findings.

Hellenistic Astrology

By the second century B.C.E., most of the elements we associate with astrology were in place.

- The horoscope, or birth-chart, gave a picture of the state of the stars at the time of a child's birth.
- The Sun, Moon, and known planets were set against the circle of the zodiac.
- There was a notion of certain zodiacal signs being *ascendant*—that is, rising over the horizon at the moment of birth.

CLASSICAL AND MEDIEVAL ASTROLOGERS

Refining the Art

The earliest notable astrologer of the Classical world was Claudius Ptolemy (90–168), also noted for his contributions to mathematics and astronomy. In fact, his system of an Earth-centered astronomy was not overturned for 1,300 years.

His chief astrological work is the *Tetrabiblos*, probably written in the Egyptian city of Alexandria, then one of the chief centers of learning in the Western world. It's very possible that Ptolemy had access to the collection of books and manuscripts maintained in the great library there, a library said to have been founded by Alexander himself. In any case, the *Tetrabiblos* draws on Babylonian and Egyptian traditions as well as Greek philosophy. Ptolemy joined astrology to medical practices, arguing that certain medicinal herbs improved their effectiveness if they were gathered during particular phases of the Moon.

Ptolemy divides the zodiac into houses, each of which is concerned with an aspect of life. In the chapters that deal with these he has a good deal to say about marriage, the quality of life, and what he regards as "diseases of the soul": greed, extravagance, stupidity, and so forth.

Manilius

Among the most important Roman astrologers was Marcus Manilius (first century). Very little is known about him; his astrological theories are contained in a long poem, of which we may not have the complete version. In the poem he denotes the signs of the zodiac:

> *First Aries shining in his golden fleece*
> *Wonders to see the back of Taurus rise,*
> *Taurus who calls, with lowered head, the Twins,*
> *Whom Cancer follows; Leo follows him,*
> *Then Virgo; Libra next, day equaling night,*
> *Draws on the Scorpion with its blazing star,*
> *Whose tail the Half-horse aims at with his bow,*
> *Ever about to loose his arrow swift.*
> *Then comes the narrow curve of Capricorn,*
> *And after him Aquarius pours from his urn*
> *Waters the following Fishes greedily use,*
> *Which Aries touches, last of all the signs.*

He also links the various signs to Roman gods: Aries to Minerva; Taurus to Venus; Gemini to Apollo; and so on.

Astrology was widely popular in the Roman world, since it was philosophically linked to Stoicism, the dominant Roman world outlook. The Stoics tended to argue that the world was governed by specific and knowable laws. From this standpoint, Manilius's line, "The fates rule the world, all things are established by settled law," was congenial to them.

The Middle Ages

The spread of Christianity in Western Europe presented problems for astrologers, since many leading Christians denounced astrology as a leftover of paganism. St. Augustine writes with regret that he continued in his youth to consult "those imposters called astrologers" but later stopped the practice after converting to Christianity. Although many medieval schools list astrology on their curricula, they apparently used the word interchangeably with astronomy.

Nonetheless, astrology was deeply rooted in popular and literary culture. When Geoffrey Chaucer (c. 1343–1400) was beginning his famous poem *The Canterbury Tales*, he wrote "and the young Sun hath in the Ram his half course run." His readers would surely have known what he was talking about.

The *Très Riche Heures*

In the fifteenth century, manuscript illuminators known as the Limburg Brothers, created a book of prayers to be spoken at the canonical hours. This beautiful work was commissioned by the Duke Berry and is known as *Très Riche Heures du Duc de Berry*. Many of its pages include zodiacal signs, although they were not used by the work to create astrological fortune telling. Rather, they are associated with the various months covered by the book.

It seems clear that despite the Church's opposition, people in the Middle Ages continued to consult horoscopes cast for them by professional astrologers, whose profession often included other forms of magical practices.

RENAISSANCE ASTROLOGERS

The Flowering of Astrology

The Renaissance is the name historians give to the revival of art and learning in Europe during the fifteenth and sixteenth centuries. It also saw a growth of astrology as a respectable—even elevated—profession, as can be seen in the lives of two of the greatest astrologers: Michel Nostradamus and John Dee.

Nostradamus

Michel Nostradamus (1503–1566) was born in Provence, France. In his youth he traveled widely, and at some point he began to cast horoscopes for those who requested them. As his reputation spread, the demand for horoscopes increased, and he took on assistants to help him. This presented challenges; Nostradamus's penmanship was poor at the best of times, and his assistants had to interpret his scribbles as best they could.

In 1555 Nostradamus published the first version of his *Prophecies*. This was a book containing collections of quatrains (four-line verses) grouped in sets of 100 (called centuries). Nostradamus continued to add to the prophecies, and by the time the last version of the book was published in 1568, there were a total of 942 quatrains (it's not entirely clear if all these were written by Nostradamus himself, but for purposes of argument, most people accept them as such).

Many of the quatrains are astrologically based; that is, they link future events to astrological influences.

> *(I:16) A scythe joined with a pond in Sagittarius*
> *at his highest ascendant*
> *Plagues, famine, death from military hands;*

the century approaches its renewal.
(I:28) Tobruk will fear the barbarian fleet for a time,
then much later the Western fleet
Cattle, people, possessions, all will be quite lost.
What a deadly combat in Tarsus and Libra.

The problem lies in interpreting these and similar verses. Nostradamus is a master of ambiguity, with the not-surprising result that over the centuries his *Prophecies* have been seen as predictors of everything from world wars to the events of 9/11.

Fake Nostradamuses

A century after Nostradamus's death, the philosopher Thomas Hobbes warned that many of the prophecies that circulated under his name were forgeries, written well after his death. Even today it's not hard to find people conveniently rewriting the prophecies to suit their already formed conclusions.

John Dee (1527–c. 1608)

Dee was among the most well-known men of his century: a scientific thinker whose reputation as an astronomer and mathematician spread throughout Europe; a mystic, astrologer, and wizard; and an advisor to the court of Elizabeth I and the queen's personal astrologer, responsible for drawing her horoscope.

Dee attended Trinity College in Cambridge (he was, in fact, a founding fellow of the school). He gained a strong scientific reputation, but sometime around then he also became known as someone who dabbled in astrological matters.

It was a difficult time in which to cast horoscopes for public figures. England had undergone an ecclesiastical reformation until Henry VIII, who, breaking from the Catholic Church, established the Church of England. This was reversed by Henry's daughter Mary, who returned the country to Catholicism and vigorously persecuted Protestants and anyone else she perceived as politically dangerous. Dee was arrested in 1555, charged with casting horoscopes for Mary and for the Princess Elizabeth, Mary's half-sister. The horoscopes, it must be presumed, predicted events not favorable to Mary. Dee succeeded in wriggling his way out of the charges, but he remained cautious during the rest of Mary's reign.

Dee prospered under Elizabeth, who came to the throne upon Mary's death in 1558. He became her official advisor on scientific questions as well as the court astrologer. In this capacity, he plunged deeper into mysticism, including astrology. He traveled extensively on the continent, but his absence from the court left him financially wanting. He died in poverty and relative obscurity about 1608.

MODERN ASTROLOGERS

Reading the Stars Today

Although after the Renaissance astrology's reputation began once again to decline, it experienced a revival in the nineteenth century with the advent of Spiritualism through people such as Madame Blavatsky (1831–1891). Spiritualism was a widespread and complex movement that involved many people, including scientists such as Alfred Russel Wallace and literary figures such as Arthur Conan Doyle. One of the changes that took place in astrology about this time is that it became simpler, in an attempt to make it more widely popular.

In the late twentieth century the growth of the New Age movement helped increase the audience for astrologers and their work. This also led to a re-evaluation of certain astrological concepts and a debate between "modern astrology" and "traditional astrology."

Some Differences Between Modern and Traditional Astrology

- Traditional astrology focuses on prediction; modern astrology is a tool for self-actualization.
- Modern astrology takes into account the nine planets of the solar system; traditional astrology relied on the seven planets that can be seen with the naked eye.
- Modern astrology takes a more "streamlined" approach to astrological investigation, showing planets in signs, houses, and aspects, rather than focusing on minute movements.
- Modern astrology often fuses with ideas from other religious or mystical traditions (e.g., Vedic astrology); traditional astrology generally stuck to Western lore.

Alan Leo (1860–1917)

Leo was one of the most influential of those astrologers who led the revival of the art in the nineteenth century. He was born William Frederick Allan (he later took his star sign as a pseudonym) in Britain.

Leo argued for a more psychologically based astrology, moving away from what he saw as the overly deterministic predictive quality of traditional astrology. He studied other spiritual traditions and attempted to integrate elements of Indian religious practice into astrology.

Dane Rudhyar (1895–1985)

Rudhyar, who was born and grew up in France, is generally credited with being the father of modern astrology. Among the chief influences on him were the writings of the psychologist C. G. Jung (1875–1961). Much of his work focused on integrating Jungian concepts into astrology. He argued that the stars do not determine our lives; rather they are images that show psychologically where we are. They don't preclude our free will and thus our ability to affect the outcome of our lives. This approach has been termed "humanistic astrology." His most important book, *The Astrology of Personality*, was published in 1936. Since the world was, at the time, thundering toward the cataclysm of the Second World War, it's understandable that the book drew limited attention. After the war, though, it gained in popularity, encouraged by its publisher, the Theosophist and mystic Alice A. Bailey (1880–1949).

It is important to understand that Rudhyar taught astrology as an active rather than a passive science. The object, he claimed, is not merely to know what the fates hold for us. Rather, astrology is a tool that enables us to probe ourselves and understand how we might fit into the greater wholeness that is the world.

THE NEW AGE MOVEMENT

Astrology in the Age of Aquarius

Alice A. Bailey, publisher of Dane Rudhyar, is often credited with the term "new age." However, regardless of the origins of the term, it has spread and is now ubiquitous. Most large bookstores have a section titled "New Age," and in many cities and towns there are specialty stores in which interested customers can purchase anything from crystals, to dowsing rods, to incense and dream catchers.

There is no question that the New Age movement has been closely aligned from its beginnings with astrology. The general assumption of the movement is that we are moving from our current age (usually called the Age of Pisces) to the Age of Aquarius, a time of enlightenment and fulfillment. (A significant statement of New Age aims was Marilyn Ferguson's *The Aquarian Conspiracy* published in 1980.)

Range of Belief

The movement has few boundaries; broadly, it seeks to see the world as a whole and to unite various strains of spiritualism, particularly those founded in Eastern thought. Among the belief systems that it embraces, astrology is an important one.

Thought Systems of the New Age Movement Include:

- Astrology
- ESP
- Existence and power of ancient civilizations: Atlantis, Lemuria, Mu, etc.
- Homeopathy
- Law of Attraction

- Near-death/after-death experiences
- Reincarnation
- Synchronicity
- Vegetarianism

The New Age movement has generally seen astrology as a way to help people discover their potential and fulfill it. As well, the movement has embraced astrology's connections to healing and to other aspects of experience such as finance, education, and love.

Sybil Leek (1917–1982)

Leek was born and raised in England, where she claimed to come from a long family line of witches. She became widely known as an advocate of witchcraft and other occult-based beliefs (she claims to have met Aleister Crowley, among the most famous of modern occultists). In the 1960s she took up astrology and shortly after moved to the United States. She became a well-known television personality, advocating for witchcraft and astrology.

New Age adherents believe the world should be comprehended as a whole, in which everything is connected to everything else. They view history as a series of great cycles, lasting 2,000 years or more. They believe we are coming to the end of one such cycle, the Age of Pisces, which included the founding of Christianity and Islam, and beginning the Age of Aquarius, characterized by love, harmony, and understanding. As can be seen from this, New Age theorists rely heavily upon astrology and astrological concepts.

CHAPTER 2

THE LANGUAGE OF ASTROLOGY

Before turning to the details of astrological predictions, we need to familiarize ourselves with some of the terms used by astrologers. Many of these are familiar to you, but they mean different things in the context of astrology.

Start with the word *astrology* itself. What does it mean?

Astrology is based on the belief that the movement of the stars and other celestial bodies affect our lives here on Earth. Not everyone acknowledges these effects, but those who study astrology have many reasons to believe that all things, both terrestrial and celestial, are strongly connected. In fact, scientists have absolutely determined that the Moon has influence over certain phenomena on Earth such as ocean tides.

One common misinterpretation of astrology is that it determines our fate. The truth, however, is that astrology describes our potential; it is our choice to live up to that potential or to deny it. Astrology is organic rather than mechanistic; its meaning grows and deepens as we learn its symbols and begin to understand its language. Astrology can't really predict what happens to us in day-to-day life because it deals with trends—not minute-to-minute occurrences.

In other words, astrology examines patterns that prevail in our lives—opportunities or gateways that are made available to us. Astrology is a highly effective way of interpreting our individual realities. The study of astrology increases our awareness and knowledge of ourselves and of the people around us. It empowers us.

SIGNS AND SYMBOLS
Our Astrological Vocabulary

Astrological signs and symbols were created for practical reasons. Consider them astrological shorthand. Once you learn about them, working with astrology and understanding astrological charts will be much easier. This understanding is important, as these charts are essential in your journey. The next three tables show the various symbols with which you should become familiar.

TABLE 1
Signs and Symbols
There are twelve signs and each has a symbol:

SIGN	SYMBOL	SIGN	SYMBOL
Aries	♈	Libra	♎
Taurus	♉	Scorpio	♏
Gemini	♊	Sagittarius	♐
Cancer	♋	Capricorn	♑
Leo	♌	Aquarius	♒
Virgo	♍	Pisces	♓

TABLE 2
Planets and Symbols

Besides the Sun and the Moon, we'll be using eight planets, two nodes, and the Part of Fortune in birth charts:

PLANET/NODE	SYMBOL	PLANET/NODE	SYMBOL
Sun	☉	Saturn	♄
Moon	☾	Uranus	♅
Mercury	☿	Neptune	♆
Venus	♀	Pluto	♇
Mars	♂	North Node	☊
Jupiter	♃	South Node	☋

TABLE 3
Aspects and Symbols

Due to the placement of planets in the houses, geometric angles are created between the planets and also between the planets and the angles of the houses. These angles are called aspects. Each aspect has a particular symbol and meaning. In this book, the following aspects are used:

ASPECT	SYMBOL	MEANING
Conjunction	☌	A separation of 0 degrees between two or more planets
Sextile	✳	A separation of 60 degrees between two or more planets
Square	□	A separation of 90 degrees between two or more planets
Trine	△	A separation of 120 degrees between two or more planets
Opposition	☍	A separation of 180 degrees between two or more planets

Other symbols used in a birth chart are:

- **Ascendant or Rising Sign (AS):** The sign and degree of the zodiac rising at the time of birth
- **Descendant (DS):** Opposite the Ascendant, cusp of the seventh house
- **Midheaven or Medium Coeli (MC):** The highest point of the zodiac at the time of birth
- **Imum Coeli or Nadir (IC):** The zodiac point opposite the Midheaven

Other symbols you'll see in the charts, but which won't be discussed in this book because they are much more complicated are:

- **Equatorial Ascendant (Eq):** The ascendant of the chart if you were born at the equator. Symbolizes who you think you are.
- **Vertex (Vtx):** A point of fate or destiny.

THE HOUSES

The Path of the Zodiac

Among the most common terms you've heard associated with astrology is "houses." You've probably heard that the zodiac is made up of twelve houses. But what exactly does this mean?

Think of the sky as a circle. Now divide it into twelve parts. Each "part" is a house. As the Sun travels over the course of a year, it makes a circle, passing from one house to the next. Your "Sun sign" is where the Sun was on the day you were born, in relation to where you were born. Your ascendant is determined by what hour and minute of the day you were born in relation to this.

On the Cusp

Because there are no "lines" in the sky dividing up the universe into precise parts, there are some discrepancies that remain in terms of determining a person's Sun sign. Those who were born at the edge of a house—during the days when one Sun changes to another—are considered to have been born "on the cusp" and may show traits from the two signs they border.

To fully understand how it all works, let's talk about the signs and their rulers. In the natural order of the zodiac, the signs begin with Aries and progress through the months to Pisces.

Part of the reason for this order that starts with Aries in Western astrology is due to the nature of the signs themselves. In astrology, we believe that Aries is the pioneer who goes out into the world first. Pisces swims through the waters of the imagination, and his dreams eventually root in the physical world and become the reality of Aries.

House Cusps

The division between one house and another is called the cusp. The sign on the ascendant sets up the structure of the various house cusps. If, for instance, you have Taurus rising—on the cusp of the first house—then Gemini sits on the cusp of your second house, Cancer on the cusp of the third, and so on around the horoscope circle.

The exception to this structure is an "intercepted sign," which means a sign that doesn't appear on the cusp of a house but is completely contained within the house.

Interceptions

Some astrologers believe an interception portends trouble for the ruler of the intercepted sign. Others think the house that holds the interception is more powerful. Actually, the outcome depends on the overall chart. Sometimes, with an interception, you're attracted to people born under the subsumed sign. Or you manifest those attributes more strongly than you might otherwise.

Each house cusp is ruled by the planet that governs the sign on the cusp. However, the natural order of the horoscope begins with Aries, then Taurus, then Gemini, and so on around the zodiac. This means that regardless of what sign is on the cusp, Mars is the natural ruler of the first house because Mars governs Aries. The attributes of the natural rulers must be taken into account when interpreting a birth chart.

MOON AND SUN SIGNS

Significant Indicators

As we'll see in Chapter 4, the planets are associated with various signs as they move through the night sky. In addition to the planets, though, there are two other important heavenly bodies that are a part of astrological lore: the Sun and the Moon. (There is, in fact, an entire branch of astrology called Lunar-Based Astrology, which we'll talk about in Chapter 4.)

For right now, all you need to know is that these two objects—the Sun and the Moon—are extremely important in understanding your charts.

Sun Signs

Your Sun sign is the pattern of your overall personality and represents your ego. The sign in which your Sun falls influences the goals you choose and how you accomplish those goals. The twelve Sun signs are divided roughly by months, but because those divisions don't follow the months exactly, you may have been born on the cusp between two signs. If you were, then read the interpretations for both signs. For instance, if you were born on April 19, the cutoff date for Aries, also read the interpretation for Taurus, because some of those attributes probably apply to you.

Generalities in your chart—using just Sun signs without Moon, ascendant, and so on—aren't wrong, but they're hardly the full story. It doesn't take into account the vast diversity inherent in every human being. However, it's a convenient way to immediately get a handle on someone you've just met.

The Nodes of the Moon

The lunar nodes are the degrees where the plane or the Moon's orbit intersects or crosses the ecliptic (Earth's orbit around the Sun). The nodes are important in the interpretation of a chart, but astrologers differ about what they mean. Astrologer Robert Hand believes that nodes "relate to connections with other people; that is, they are an axis of relationship. In this context, the North Node has a joining quality, while the South has a separating quality."

Northern and Southern Nodes

In Hindu astrology, both nodes are considered to be malefic ("bad"). In Western astrology, the North Node, called the Dragon's Head, is considered an easier aspect, the equivalent of Jupiter, and the South Node, or Dragon's Tail, is considered the equivalent of Saturn.

Another theory ties the nodes in with reincarnation. In this theory, the South Node represents our karma, deeply embedded patterns of behavior and thought we acquired in previous lives. We need to overcome these patterns through the North Node, which represents the area of our most profound growth in this life.

In *The Inner Sky*, astrologer Steven Forrest writes: "the South Node of the Moon symbolizes our karma . . . it shows a kind of behavior that is instinctive and automatic . . . it speaks of mindset and a pattern of motivations that arise spontaneously." "The North Node," according to Forrest, "represents the point that puts the most unrelenting tension on the past. As we allow ourselves to experience it, we open up to an utterly alien and exotic reality. We are stretched to the breaking point."

Bias and Expansion

Constant dependence on karma implies denial of free will. Instead, think of the South Node as an unconscious bias—either from previous incarnations or that which builds up during our lives. It's what we need to release in order to grow. The North Node sign and house placement indicate the area of our lives we need to expand so we can evolve toward our fulfillment as spiritual beings.

Sometimes, the nodes seem to work in a symbiotic relationship with Saturn. As we encounter restrictions in the area where Saturn sits in our chart, we are seemingly forced to rid ourselves of South Node prejudices by working through our North Node energies. The North Node also represents the types of people we gravitate toward, and the South Node represents the types of people we avoid.

CHAPTER 3

ASTROLOGY'S HOUSES

Houses are fundamental to an understanding of astrology. In this chapter you'll learn about the attributes of each house and how to read them on charts.

The first thing we'll consider is Sun signs. Remember, these are where the Sun was on the day you were born. They play a key role in indicating your personality.

During the 1960s, when astrology enjoyed a boom unlike anything it had known since the late 1800s, it seemed that everyone knew everyone else's Sun sign—even if no one knew exactly what it meant. A Gemini was pegged as bright and fun, flighty and flirtatious, but basically two-faced and superficial. Virgos were known as being fussy about details. In this chapter, the descriptions of Sun signs are broken down into six sections: women, men, work, finances, physical traits, and spirituality.

ARIES

The Ram (March 21–April 20)

Element: Fire
Quality: Cardinal
Keywords: Leadership, the pioneer spirit
Planetary Ruler: Mars
Rules: Head and face; natural ruler of first house

Aries are bold, courageous, and resourceful. They always seem to know what they believe, what they want from life, and where they're going. Aries people are dynamic and aggressive (sometimes, to a fault) in pursuing their goals. They're also survivors.

The challenge with this sign is lack of persistence: Aries people sometimes lose interest if they don't see rapid results. But this tendency is compensated for by their ambition and drive to succeed. They can be argumentative, lack tact, and have bad tempers. On the other hand, their anger rarely lasts long, and they can be warm and loving with those they care about.

Aries Woman

Don't offend or anger an Aries woman. If you do, she'll never forget it, and you won't see much of her after that. She'll turn her energy to someone or something else. If you're involved with an Aries woman, the relationship had better be one of equality, or she won't stick around. This isn't a woman who tolerates chauvinism.

Professionally, she's driven. She sets goals and pursues them with all the relentless energy she possesses. She's great at initiating projects, launching ideas, and putting things into action. But she isn't particularly good at seeing a project or idea through to its completion unless she passionately believes in it. She can hold her own in most situations and certainly can compete with any man on the professional front. She exudes an aura of success and dresses to enhance that aura.

Aries Man

This man is as bold and brash as his female counterpart and just as impatient and driven. Thanks to his innate courage, he may take up daredevil sports. He wants to prove himself and takes unnecessary chances and risks.

He's a man who relies on his own judgment and intuition to make decisions. Like the female Aries, he projects a successful image even if he has failed at some endeavors in the past.

He's Never Boring

Some women may find the Aries man too audacious for their tastes, but life with him is never boring. If he's got the money, he will absolutely spend it all. And no one is as creative as the Aries man when it comes to wooing a woman.

Once an Aries man is smitten, watch out. He brings his considerable energy to the relationship and pursues the woman in a whirlwind of romance. But if the emotion isn't reciprocated quickly, he'll be gone in a flash. On the other hand, if it is—and he falls out of love—he'll be out the door before a woman can even try to convince him to stay. He's not easily talked into or out of something. Once he makes up his mind, it's usually a done deal.

Famous Aries

- Abigail Breslin
- Adolf Hitler
- Celine Dion
- Danica Patrick
- Heath Ledger
- Leonardo da Vinci
- Quentin Tarantino
- Seth Rogen
- Victoria Beckham

Work

An Aries excels at anything in which leadership ability is paramount. These people like giving orders, and they're terrific at delegating responsibilities. They have numerous ideas and want to put them all into effect yesterday. As a fire sign, they pour energy into whatever they do. They aren't particularly interested in having power over others. They simply want the power to do what they want without restriction.

Finances

An Aries knows something should be tucked away, but retirement seems such a long way off. And besides, money always comes in when needed! The challenge for an Aries is to develop the habit of saving.

Head-Based Ailments

Since Aries rules the head and face, these areas are considered to be the weakest parts of the body for them. Common ailments are tension headaches, dizziness, and skin eruptions. In fact, many Aries suffer from migraines and allergies, too. Also, because they're indulgent, Aries need to be careful of easily gaining weight.

Spirituality

Aries is likely to sample a little of everything before deciding on which spiritual belief fits best. He might live in an ashram, delve into paganism, or even try out a more conventional religion. While involved with a particular spiritual path, he will be passionate about it. But unless his passion is sustained, an Aries will eventually get bored and move on to something new.

TAURUS

The Bull (April 21–May 20)

Element: Earth
Quality: Fixed
Keywords: Endurance, perseverance, stubbornness
Planetary Ruler: Venus
Rules: Neck, throat, cervical vertebrae; natural ruler of second house

While Aries is out pioneering and discovering new lands, Taurus is settling and cultivating the land and using his resources for practical purposes. His stubbornness and determination keep him around for the long haul on any project or endeavor.

Taurus is the most stubborn sign in the zodiac. Taureans are also patient, singular in their pursuit of goals, and determined to attain what they want. They compensate for lack of versatility by enduring whatever they have to in order to get what they want. Long after other contestants have fallen out of the race, Taurus individuals are still in the running. As a result, they often succeed where others fail.

Most Taureans enjoy being surrounded by nice things. They like fine art and music, and many have considerable musical ability. They also have a talent for working with their hands—gardening, woodworking, and sculpting.

It takes a lot to anger a Taurus person, but once you do, clear out. The "bull's rush" can be fierce. But thanks to Venus ruling this sign, Taurus people are usually sensual and romantic. They are also physically oriented individuals who take pride in their bodies.

Taurus Woman

She's loyal and dedicated to whatever she loves most. Her central interests reflect her particular tastes in art, color, and decor. She enjoys beauty, whatever its guise. If she's into clothing, then she dresses well and tastefully. If sports and physical activity are her passion, she pursues them diligently and with tremendous patience.

Courting a Taurean Woman

Since the Taurus woman is Venus-ruled, she's a romantic. Court her with flowers, moonlit walks on the beach, and poetry. She's a generous, ardent lover, who probably has a love of music. She may even play an instrument or sing. If you want to change her opinion on something, though, go about it in a gentle way. Don't ever back her into a corner. She'll dig in her heels and refuse to budge!

As an Earth sign, she likes to putter in the garden and perhaps grows and cultivates herbs. She benefits from any time spent outdoors doing something she finds pleasurable. Animals are important to her and if she has pets, they reflect her own tastes in beauty.

Taurus Man

Like his female counterpart, the Taurus man works hard and patiently at what he loves. His patience and perseverance make him good at finishing what other people have started. This guy isn't impetuous. Considerable thought goes into most things that he does. It's not that he's cautious; he's merely purposeful. If he doesn't understand the reason for doing something, he won't do it, and nothing you say will change his mind.

Massage the Taurean Man

Taurus's romantic nature may not always show up in flowers and gifts, but he does others things that tell you he cares. In return, he enjoys a good massage; likes having his neck rubbed; and adores sitting with a nice glass of wine and his honey in front of a fireplace.

Both men and women in this sign can be jealous and possessive. But this tendency is mitigated considerably if the Taurus man knows you're as sincere as he is. He may have a deep connection with nature and the natural world that manifests in camping and solo sports. If he works out in a gym, he probably does it alone, without a trainer. He may be into yoga, alternative medicine, and health foods.

Famous Tauruses

- Billy Joel
- Charlotte Brontë
- George Lucas
- Harry S. Truman
- Karl Marx
- Madeleine Albright
- Pierce Brosnan
- Queen Elizabeth II
- Tori Spelling
- Uma Thurman

Work

Taureans excel at work that requires persistence, stability, and relentless drive. They're able to take abstract ideas and make them concrete and practical. This means they're good at behind-the-scenes work, especially if the work is artistically creative—writing, costume design, gourmet cooking, musical composition, or anything to do with nature. You won't find a more tireless worker in the zodiac.

Finances

Despite the Taurean need for material security, they enjoy spending money. But the spending is rarely frivolous because Taurean tastes are quite specific and usually refined. Books, art, travel, and shamanic workshops may offer security for the Taurus.

Spirituality

Taurus, due to the fixed, Earth temperament of the sign, often seeks spiritual answers in nature. While camping, hiking, or engaging in some sort of physical activity outside, she connects with the deeper levels of self. Music and the arts can have the same effect on a Taurus.

GEMINI

The Twins (May 21–June 21)

Element: Air
Quality: Mutable
Keyword: Versatility
Planetary Ruler: Mercury
Rules: Hands, arms, lungs, nervous system; natural ruler of the third house

After Aries and Taurus have discovered and cultivated new land, Geminis venture out to see what else is there and seize upon new ideas that will expand their communities. Their innate curiosity keeps these people on the move.

Geminis, because they're ruled by Mercury, tend to use the rational, intellectual mind to explore and understand their personal worlds. They need to answer the single burning question in their minds: Why? This applies to most facets of their lives, from the personal to the impersonal. This need to know may send them off to foreign countries, particularly if the Sun is in the ninth house, where their need to explore other cultures and traditions ranks high.

The Changeable Gemini

Geminis are changeable and often moody! Their symbol, the twins, means they are often at odds with themselves—the mind demanding one thing, the heart demanding the opposite. As a Gemini's significant other, you might reach a point where you wonder which twin you're with!

These individuals are fascinated by relationships and connections among people, places, and objects. Their rational analysis of everything, from ideas to relationships, drives them as crazy as it drives everyone else around them. When this quality leads them into an exploration of psychic and spiritual realms, it grounds them. In romance, the heart of a Gemini is won by seduction of the mind.

Gemini Woman

At first glance, she seems to be all over the place. She can talk on any number of topics and sounds like she knows what she's talking about, until you discover that her knowledge on most things is, alas, superficial. But if you hit on one of her passions, her knowledge is deep and thorough. She excels at communication; the form this talent takes depends on other aspects in her chart.

In her twenties, she tends to be flirtatious and flighty, unable or unwilling to commit to a relationship. On the one hand, this girl loves her freedom; on the other, relationships are important to her. If she marries young, she may marry at least twice. In her thirties and forties, she begins to settle in. By this time, she has made a kind of peace with herself. She has a better understanding of her moods, needs, and emotions. By fifty, the Gemini woman knows who she is; now she must begin living that truth.

If you want to change this woman's attitude or opinion, you have to prove that your attitude or opinion is more logical. Remember that her concept of logic may differ from yours.

Gemini Man

He's quick, witty, and enigmatic. Just when you think you've got him figured out, he says or does something that blows your concept of who he is. Don't expect a courtship from this guy; he doesn't possess the sensual appreciation of beauty that a Taurus man has. But if you appeal to his intellect—if you court him mentally—he might dedicate his next book to you.

Solving the Gemini Man Riddle?

Like his female counterpart, the Gemini man often seems to be two people inhabiting one body. One twin is attentive to your every need and whim. But the other twin couldn't care less. You won't change this particular quality. It's inherent. You simply have to get accustomed to it.

The Gemini man makes a good editor, writer, or orator. He may hold down two jobs and is certainly capable of working on more than one project at a time. Once he commits to something though, whether it's a profession or a relationship, he needs to know that he is appreciated.

Famous Geminis
- Anderson Cooper
- Angelina Jolie
- Bob Dylan
- Henry Kissinger
- Joe Montana
- Marilyn Monroe
- Martha Washington
- Sally Ride
- Shia LaBeouf
- Suze Orman

Work

Geminis excel in any line of work that provides diversity. It doesn't matter if it's with the public or behind the scenes, as long as it isn't routine. They make good counselors because one of the twins is always willing to listen. Their love of language gives them a talent for the written word. Acting, politics, libraries, research: all these fields fit Gemini. Boredom to a Gemini is like death.

Finances

How a Gemini handles money depends on which of the twins holds the purse strings at the time—the spendthrift or the tightwad. Either way, Geminis enjoy spending money on the things they love, such as books, movies, theater, and travel.

Spirituality

Geminis are so restless mentally that they generally don't do well within organized religions, unless they've chosen that path for themselves. They sample spiritual belief systems the way other people sample new foods. However, once a Gemini finds a spiritual path that makes sense, she generally sticks with it.

CANCER

The Crab (June 22–July 22)

Element: Water
Quality: Cardinal
Keywords: Nurturing, emotional drive
Planetary Ruler: Moon
Rules: Breasts, stomach, digestive system; natural ruler of the fourth house

Imagination, sensitivity, and the nurturing instinct characterize this sign. Cancerians are generally gentle and kind people, unless they're hurt. Then they can become vindictive and sharp-spoken. They forgive easily, but rarely forget. Cancerians tend to be affectionate, passionate, and even possessive at times. As parents, they may be over-protective. As spouses or significant others, they may smother their mates with love and good intentions.

Moving Sideways

Emotionally, Cancerians act and react in the same way the crab moves—sideways. They avoid confrontations and usually aren't comfortable in discussing what they feel. They're reluctant to reveal who they are and sometimes hide behind their protective urges, preferring to tend to the needs of others rather than to their own needs.

Cancers are intuitive and can sometimes be psychic. They're often moody and always changeable; their interests and social circles shift constantly. Once a Cancer trusts you, however, he lets you in on his most private world.

Cancer Woman

At first she seems enigmatic, elusive. She's so changeable in her moods that you never know where you stand with her. Beneath her gentle and sympathetic nature, beneath her bravado, she's scared of being pinned down and insecure about who she is.

Cancers and Children

If a Cancer woman doesn't have children of her own, she probably has some sort of connection with children. Animals or people in need are like her own children—she likes to extend herself emotionally. Somehow, her nurturing instinct finds expression through giving to other living things, including plants.

She needs roots—her own home, preferably near water—where she can establish a base. She nurtures everything—animals, her own children, waifs, and orphans of all shapes, sizes, and species. This woman is emotion distilled into its purest form. She feels first, then thinks.

Cancer Man

Like the female Cancer, the male has expressive eyes that communicate a kind of forlorn nostalgia for things past. He's kind, affectionate, and nurturing, but only to a point. When he feels his personal space has been infringed upon, he retreats just like the crab—rapidly to the side. Then he buries himself in sand by retreating to his special place—his own home. Like the female Cancer, he is often nurturing and gets along well with children.

This guy is hard to figure out. Sometimes he courts you with flowers and candlelight; other times he's sacked out on the couch lost in his own gloom. Your best course of action is to let him be. Don't prod him when he's in this kind of mood. You won't get anywhere with him even if you do.

If he's interested in spiritual issues, chances are he's in deep. In this sign, you're likely to find psychic healers and clairvoyants—people who use their intuition in highly developed and sophisticated ways.

Famous Cancers

- Alan Turing
- Camilla Parker Bowles
- George W. Bush
- Ginger Rogers
- Harrison Ford
- Jesse Ventura
- Kathy Bates
- Lindsay Lohan
- Michael Phelps

Work

Cancerians may be happiest when they work from their own homes. Due to the intensity of their feelings, they do well in medicine, working directly with patients. For the same reason, they also make good psychic healers, counselors, and psychologists. Teaching children, publicity and marketing, being involved in sociology or anthropology, running a daycare center, or even taking care of other people's homes are also good fits for the Cancerian personality.

Finances

Cancers aren't lavish spenders except when it comes to their homes and families. Then, nothing is too expensive. Otherwise, they tend to be big savers. As teens, they stash their allowance in cookie jars; as adults, they stick their money in long-term CDs.

Spirituality

Introspection is the key with Cancers, and it doesn't matter if it's provided in the guise of organized religion or an alternative belief system. When they feel a particular set of beliefs is a fit, they stick with it, explore it, and draw upon their innate intuition to understand it.

LEO

The Lion (July 23–August 22)

Element: Fire
Quality: Fixed
Keywords: Action, power
Planetary Ruler: Sun
Rules: Heart, back, and spinal cord; natural ruler of the fifth house

Leos roar. They love being the center of attention and often surround themselves with admirers. To remain in the proud kingdom of a Leo, her admirers have to think like she thinks, believe what she believes, and hate and love whom she hates and loves. To a Leo, this is loyalty. In return, Leo offers generosity, warmth, and compassion.

Leos have an innate dramatic sense, and life is their stage. Their flamboyance and personal magnetism extend to every facet of their lives. They seek to succeed and make an impact in every situation. It is no surprise that the theater and allied arts fall under the rule of Leo.

Leo Woman

She's up front about what she feels and invariably is disappointed when she finds that other people may not be as forthright. You'll never have to guess where you stand with a Leo woman unless there's something in the aspects of her chart that says otherwise. She can't "pretend." She can be diplomatic, but, if her heart isn't in it, she isn't capable of deceiving someone into thinking it is. She loves flattery and over-the-top romantic courtships. She is an ardent lover.

Loyal Leos

The Leo woman exudes confidence, and because of this, other people place their trust in her. And that's no mistake: Leo is loyal, to a fault. She needs to be at the helm in her workplace—a managerial position will do, but CEO would be better. She dislikes playing second fiddle on any level and would rather work from home than have to contend with working for employers whom she doesn't respect.

In a marriage, don't expect her to be content with staying home, unless she's running her business from there. If she's a mother, she's not just a mother. She has a career, hobbies, and passions. Because Leo also rules children, she may be involved somehow with children, even if she doesn't have her own.

She likes nice clothes and probably dresses with flair and style in bright, bold colors. Remember that she's an actress and adept at creating certain impressions and moods through the way she looks and acts. She's a chameleon. She likes order in her world, but it has to be her order.

Leo Man

Give him center stage, and he's at his best; tell him what to do, and he's at his worst. Once you accept that about the Leo man, he's easy to get along with because you really want to like this guy. He's warm, outgoing, and fun. Kids love him because in many ways he's like they are—full of magic.

People are attracted to him because they sense his leadership abilities. They like his frankness, abundant energy, and ambition. If you're a Leo's significant other, get used to sharing him with his "court." Rest assured, though, that if your Leo commits to you, he means it.

Famous Leos

- Alfred Hitchcock
- Amelia Earhart
- Fidel Castro
- H.P. Lovecraft
- Jennifer Lopez
- John Stamos
- Louis Vuitton
- Lucille Ball
- Whitney Houston
- Zelda Fitzgerald

Work

A Leo excels at work in front of the public. He's a great actor, orator, Speaker of the House, or CEO—a menial job won't do. Leos are good at teaching because the classroom becomes their stage, and their students become their audience. They make excellent writers, editors, and journalists. They also tend to be good with animals and enjoy training, caring for, and loving them.

Finances

If Leo wants it, Leo buys it. If he can't afford it, he charges it. If his charge cards are maxed out, then he hocks his Rolex or his collection of baseball cards to buy it. Saving for a rainy day just isn't in the picture because, for a Leo, there aren't any rainy days! There are, of course, exceptions to all these generalities. A Moon in an Earth sign, combined with a Leo Sun, would mitigate the flamboyance, particularly if the Moon were in Capricorn. But these are just details.

Spirituality

Most Leos were probably once Sun-worshipping pagans in past lives. Now they're sampling everything else along the spectrum. Unless aspects in the chart indicate otherwise, a Leo isn't likely to stay within the confines of organized religion unless it suits him. If he does it out of obligation, then, in his mind, he's doing it for his kids. A Leo's greatest spiritual contribution comes when he expands beyond the parameters of the self and reaches for the universal.

VIRGO

The Virgin (August 23–September 22)

Element: Earth
Quality: Mutable
Keywords: Order, detailed, dedication
Planetary Ruler: Mercury
Rules: Intestines, abdomen, female reproductive system; natural ruler of the sixth house

Virgos are like Geminis in terms of mental quickness and agility. Due to their attention to detail, they tend to delve more deeply into subjects they study. Even though they are career-oriented people, they seem to be more interested in doing their jobs efficiently and well. They're happiest when engaged in something that benefits society at large. In other words, duty is important to Virgos.

Stimulating Relationships

Virgos tend to be attracted to people who are intellectually stimulating or eccentric in some way. Their standards are high when it comes to romantic relationships, and unless the mental connection exists, the relationship won't last long. In their twenties, many Virgos find critical partners or those who don't appreciate them fully—an unhealthy match.

Since Virgos, like Geminis, are Mercury-ruled, they need outlets for all their nervous energy. Running, martial arts, or workouts at the gym are recommended. Writing, pets, reading, and extra education can also serve this purpose.

Virgo Woman

She possesses a certain vibrancy and energy that other people sense even when she's not trying to project an image. In romance, she is attracted first when a mental spark exists. As the mental camaraderie deepens, so do her emotions.

The Virgo woman, like her male counterpart, is often insecure and tends to fret over everything. This trait usually evens out as the Virgo woman matures. It can be irritating to a significant other, particularly when her fretting turns to a constant critique of everything other people say and do.

Virgos on the Cutting Edge

A Virgo woman is usually aware of health and hygiene issues, especially when it concerns cutting-edge research. She may not always apply what she knows to her own life, but she has the knowledge. She's also aware of the world and pays attention to business and political issues.

A Virgo woman enjoys spending money on items like books and pieces of art that strike her fancy. She's sensitive to her surroundings, so her home is always comfortable. If she's a mother, she's conscientious, tactful, and loving. She usually has a soft spot for animals, too.

Virgo Man

He looks good and possesses an indisputable presence. He's mentally quick, intellectually curious, and is an excellent worker. His humor is often biting but rarely malicious.

He can be fussy about his personal environment. If he cooks, then he probably is quite good at it and possessive about the kitchen while he's creating. Like the female of the sign, the Virgo man enjoys pleasant surroundings and usually owns several special items that he keeps for nostalgia's sake.

He's prone to taking himself too seriously and benefits from any activity that forces him to lighten up. He's always hardest on himself, overly critical of what he does or doesn't do and can be quite critical of others as well. He rarely seeks praise for his efforts.

Famous Virgos
- Adam Sandler
- Amy Poehler
- B.B. King
- Bill Murray
- Colin Firth
- Jimmy Fallon
- Mary Shelley
- Pink
- Stella McCartney

Work

Virgos sincerely strive for perfection in their work and careers. They do best when working for others—social work, in hospitals, clinics, hospice programs, or with their children. The challenge in every area of a Virgo's life is to serve without self-sacrifice. Their striving for perfection compels them to evolve and change.

Finances

When Virgos are big spenders, they usually pull back at some critical point and question what they buy and why. What need does it fill? If they are tight with money, then something happens that impels them to loosen their hold—to spend money for enjoyment. Virgos follow an arc of evolution toward perfection in everything they do. They analyze patterns in their lives and seek to change those that don't work.

Spirituality

The evolved Virgo is capable of great vision and an intuition that often borders on prescience. They are likely to sample different spiritual beliefs until they find one that appeals to their eminently practical side.

LIBRA

The Scales (September 23–October 22)

Element: Air
Quality: Cardinal
Keyword: Balance
Planetary Ruler: Venus
Rules: Lower back and the diaphragm; natural ruler of the seventh house

The typical Libra seeks to mediate and balance. Librans have an inherent need to act democratically, diplomatically, and fairly—always.

Libras in Love

In love, Libras are natural romantics and flourish in enduring partnerships. They are fair-minded people, but avoid anything that is grim, crude, vulgar, or garish. Adversely afflicted, they have trouble making decisions and may lose themselves in sensual pleasures. In highly evolved Librans, the human mind finds the perfect blend between balance and discretion.

They love beauty in all its guises—art, literature, classical music, opera, mathematics, and the human body. They usually are team players who enjoy debate but not argument. They're excellent strategists and masters at the power of suggestion. They use diplomacy and intelligence to get what they want.

Libra Woman

Watch out: She's a flirt who is seductive and romantic, and she bowls you over with the small luxuries she brings you. If she cooks, she probably does it well, using herbs and seasonings. She sets the mood, too, with candlelight, fresh flowers, and soft music. She's a romantic, tender lover who enjoys companionship and flourishes in partnerships.

Her home reflects her refined tastes in art, books, and good music. She may not be extravagant and probably doesn't squander the money she has, but she derives enormous pleasure from whatever she buys. If she likes opera or the ballet, she attends regularly; these extravagances feed her soul. She may play a musical instrument and may have a fondness for chess.

Libra Man

He needs companionship, just like his female counterpart, and generally works better as part of a team. But he also needs to retain his individuality in any partnership, which may be quirky at times. Once you've won his heart, he's loyal and considerate and seeks to perfect the union until it fits his idealized vision of what is possible.

He enjoys pleasant, harmonious surroundings in his work and personal environment. He often finds himself in the role of peacemaker because he seeks balance in all things. He shares many of the same artistic interests as his female counterpart.

Anger Avoidance

A Libra man rarely expresses anger. He'd rather work around whatever problems crop up. But if he lets loose, he leaves nothing unsaid! Every transgression and hurt is spelled out. Although his anger passes quickly, such outbursts leave him shaken and sometimes ill because he has such an intense dislike for anything unpleasant!

Famous Libras

- Al Yankovic
- Daniel Boone
- Hugh Jackman
- Jimmy Carter
- Julie Andrews
- Kim Kardashian
- Mahatma Gandhi
- Sharon Osbourne
- Susan Sarandon
- Toni Braxton

Work

The Libra's obvious choice for a profession is attorney or judge because of his finely tuned sense of fair play. Librans generally excel in any profession that calls for an acutely balanced mind and sensitivities. They make good editors, musicians, accountants, artists, and parents. The work itself is less important than what it teaches Libras about making decisions, in spite of their ability to see all sides of an issue.

Finances

A sense of balance allows Libras to strike the right note between spender and miser. Libras tend to save, but they enjoy spending when they can afford it. Most Libras know their limit.

Spirituality

Evolved Libras understand instinctively that they must unite human duality with divine unity. They seek idealized balance; the perfect equilibrium. For some, this is accomplished within the parameters of organized religion. For others, spirituality is sought through community efforts or in their immediate family.

SCORPIO

The Scorpion (October 23–November 21)

Element: Water
Quality: Fixed
Keywords: Regeneration, transformation
Planetary Ruler: Mars and Pluto
Rules: Sexual organs, rectum, and reproductive system; natural ruler of the eighth house

Note the sharp point at the tip of the glyph that represents this sign. Symbolically, it's the scorpion's stinger, which characterizes the biting sarcasm often associated with Scorpios. These people are intense, passionate, and strong-willed. They often impose their will on others. In less aware people, this can manifest as cruelty, sadism, and enmity; in the more evolved Scorpio, this characteristic transforms lives for the better. Like Aries, Scorpios aren't afraid of anything. They plow ahead and overcome whatever opposition they encounter.

No Gray Areas

Scorpios don't know the meaning of indifference. They either approve or disapprove, agree or disagree. You're either a friend or an enemy: there are no shades of gray. Once you've gained a Scorpio's trust, you've won his loyalty forever—unless you hurt him or someone he loves. Then they can become vindictive enemies.

Scorpios possess an innate curiosity and suspicion of easy answers that compels them to probe deeply into whatever interests them. They dig out concealed facts and seek the meaning behind facades. Most Scorpios are exceptionally intuitive, even if they don't consciously acknowledge it. The more highly evolved people in this sign are often very psychic, with rich inner lives and passionate involvement in metaphysics.

Scorpios are excellent workers: industrious and relentless. They excel at anything associated with the eighth house—trusts and inheritances, mortuaries, psychological counselors, and the occult. Sometimes they're more passionate with their work than they are with the important people in their lives.

Scorpio Woman

She smolders with sexuality. This is a woman who turns heads on the street, who walks into a room filled with strangers and instantly grabs attention through nothing more than the power of her presence. If you seek to win a Scorpio woman's heart, you'd better be up front and honest right from the beginning. If she ever catches you in a lie or if you hurt her, she'll cut you off cold.

She's a passionate lover and can be jealous and possessive. You won't ever figure out what she's thinking or feeling just by the expression on her face, unless she's angry—then watch out! Her rage takes many forms—an explosion, sarcasm that bites to the bone, or a piercing look that makes you shrivel inside.

If her intuition is developed, it borders on clairvoyance. This inner sense often shines forth in a Scorpio woman's striking eyes. As a mother, the Scorpio woman is devoted, loving, and fiercely protective. She strives to create a comfortable and loving home for her kids that can also be a refuge from the outside world.

NAME

Velarde, Nevaeh

BIRTH DATE   COUNSELOR   B - G   YR. GRAD.

PASS TO LEAVE SCHOOL GROUNDS

DESTINATION   Dr. Appt

REASON FOR LEAVING   Meet in front

per mom

X _____   _____
SIGNATURE OF PARENT, DOCTOR, STORE, ETC.   TIME   DATE

I-PP-10   HAYWARD UNIFIED SCHOOL DISTRICT

5-5-19
TIME 12:30 DATE
Mills PERIOD
SCHOOL

Scorpio Man

Like the female of the sign, he's intense, passionate, and very private. There is always something compelling about a Scorpio man—his eyes, the way he dresses, or the enigma of his presence. He isn't just a flirt. He often comes on like a locomotive with sexual energy, radiating so powerfully that he's difficult to ignore even if you aren't attracted to him.

The Scorpio man often has a marvelous talent of some kind that he pursues passionately, but which may not figure into his income. In other words, his talent is his avocation—music, art, writing, acting, astrology, or tarot cards. Or, he may pour his considerable talent into nurturing his own children.

Many Scorpio men (and women) enjoy sports. They have a distinct preference for more violent sports like football and hunting. Their choice of sports is sometimes a reflection of a personal struggle with emotional extremes.

Famous Scorpios

- Anne Hathaway
- Charles Manson
- Ethan Hawke
- Gordon Ramsay
- Jimmy Kimmel
- Laura Bush
- Natalie Merchant
- Peter Jackson
- Scarlett Johansson
- Whoopi Goldberg

Work

They make excellent actors, detectives, spies, even teachers. There's just no telling where all that rawness of perception can take a Scorpio. One thing's for sure, though—his work follows his passion.

Finances

Scorpios are masters at using other people's money to build their own fortunes. In return, Scorpios can be extravagantly generous in charity work or anonymous donors to worthy causes. Your Scorpio may even rewrite the last act of your rejected screenplay and get it to sell big-time.

Spirituality

Some Scorpios take to organized religion like a duck to water. They like the ritual and the sense of belonging. Others, however, delve into unorthodox belief systems seeking spiritual answers. Whatever form spirituality takes for a Scorpio, he or she brings passion and sincerity to the search.

SAGITTARIUS

The Archer (November 22–December 21)

Element: Fire
Quality: Mutable
Keywords: Idealism, freedom
Planetary Ruler: Jupiter
Rules: Hips, thighs, liver, and hepatic system; natural ruler of the ninth house

These people seek the truth, express it as they see it—and don't care if anyone else agrees with them. They see the large picture of any issue and can't be bothered with the mundane details. They are always outspoken and can't understand why other people aren't as candid. After all, what is there to hide?

For this sign logic reigns supreme. But the mentality differs from Gemini, the polar opposite of Sagittarius, in several important ways. A Gemini is concerned with the here and now: he needs to know how and why things and relationships work in his life. A Sagittarian, however, focuses on the future and on the larger family of humanity. Quite often, this larger family includes animals—large, small, wild, or domestic—and the belief that all deserve the right to live free.

Despite Sagittarians' propensity for logic, they often possess an uncanny ability to glimpse the future. Even when they have this ability, however, they often think they need external tools to trigger it, such as tarot cards, an astrology chart, or runes. However, many Sagittarians reject the idea of astrology, as well—they rely solely on practicality and inherent intuition.

They love their freedom and chafe at any restrictions. Their versatility and natural optimism win them many friends, but only a few ever really know the heart of the Sagittarian.

Sagittarius Woman

She's hard to figure out at first. You see her in a crowd and notice that she commands attention. She's humorous, vivacious, and outspoken. One on one, she's flirtatious. But the moment you mention having dinner or catching a movie, she's gone. It's not that she's coy; it's simply that you're just a face in the crowd.

Talk Fast

If you catch Sagittarius woman's attention, it's because you talk well and quickly about something that interests her. Animal rights, for instance, or paradigm shifts in worldwide belief systems, will definitely be topics of concern. This lady thinks big and if you want to win her heart, you'd better think just as big.

Sagittarian women excel in jobs and careers that don't confine them. If they have children, they allow their offspring such latitude that to other people it may appear that they're indifferent. This is hardly the case. A Sagittarian mother is loving and devoted, but believes that her children should find their own way. She offers broad guidelines and her own wisdom but doesn't force her opinions.

Sagittarius Man

He's a charmer, flirtatious and witty; the kind of man everyone loves to have at a party. He's also candid and opinionated, with firm ideas on how things work and should be done. His frustration is that ideas that often seem so obvious to him, seem oblique to other people.

His vision is broad and often grandiose. He does everything in a big way and is rarely satisfied with what he achieves. On his way to attaining a particular goal, he gets carried away with the momentum he has built up and ends up taking on more than he can handle.

The less evolved men of this sign sometimes lose sight of the difference between need and greed. They want everything, and they want it immediately. This is as true in business as it is in romance. Sagittarian men often have more than one relationship going on at a time, which suits their need for freedom. For this reason, Sagittarius is also known as the bachelor sign.

Famous Sagittarians
- Alyssa Milano
- Baruch Spinoza
- Frank Zappa
- Miley Cyrus
- Pope Francis
- Ralph Fiennes
- Samuel L. Jackson
- Sarah Silverman
- Tina Turner
- Vanessa Hudgens

Work

Constraint isn't in the Sagittarian vocabulary. Or, when it is, the word and the reality influence other people's lives, not the Sagittarian's. They work best in jobs and fields where they have complete freedom to call the shots: an owner of an airline, CEO, small business owner, entrepreneur, actor, writer, or traveling salesperson. The point isn't the work so much as the freedom of the work.

Finances

A Sagittarius has plenty of options about where to spend his or her money—travel, education, workshops, seminars, animals, or books—and that's often the problem. How can they narrow their choices? What should they buy first? More than likely, they will toss all their choices into the air and seize the one that hits the ground first.

Spirituality

As the natural ruler of the ninth house, which governs philosophy, religion, and higher education, Sagittarians generally sample a vast array of spiritual beliefs. Once they find a belief system that suits them, they generally stick with it. In this way, they are much like their polar opposite, Gemini. The difference, though, is that Sagittarius delves more deeply into spiritual matters.

CAPRICORN

The Goat (December 22–January 19)

Element: Earth
Quality: Cardinal
Keywords: Materialism, self-discipline
Planetary Ruler: Saturn
Rules: Knees, skin, and bones; natural ruler of the tenth house

Capricorns are serious-minded people who often seem aloof and tightly in control of their emotions and their personal domain. Even as youngsters, there's a mature air about them, as if they were born with a profound core that few outsiders ever see.

This sign's nickname, the goat, represents Capricorn's slow, steady rise through the world. They're easily impressed by outward signs of success, but are interested less in money than in the power that money represents. Like Scorpio, they feel the need to rule whatever kingdom they occupy whether this is their home, workplace, or business. Like Scorpios, they prize power and mastery over others, but they tend to be subtler about it.

Capricorns are true workers—industrious, efficient, and disciplined. They deplore inertia in other people. Their innate common sense gives them the ability to plan ahead and to work out practical ways of approaching goals. More often than not, they succeed at whatever they set out to do.

Worriers

They're natural worriers. Even when they've taken all the precautions they can possibly take, Capricorns fret that they've forgotten something. They can benefit from the idea of "perfect faith"—that whatever they do will work out fine. Unfortunately, they're hard to convince of that.

In a crowd, Capricorns aren't particularly easy to spot. They aren't physically distinctive, and they aren't the life of the party. But they possess a quiet dignity that's unmistakable.

Capricorn Woman

At first glance, she appears to be tough as nails—a determined, serious woman who seems to know where she has been, where she is, and where she's going. But when you get to know her, you'll discover she's not tough at all—she's merely guarded and reserved. Don't expect her to welcome you into her life with open arms. You have to prove yourself first.

Dominant Capricorns

As a mother, she's devoted and often runs her home with the efficiency of a business. Due to the Saturn influence on this sign, the Capricorn woman can sometimes be too rigid with her spouse and children. She expects a lot and, supported by other aspects in her chart, may enforce her will to the point of dominance.

This woman has certain parameters and boundaries that she won't cross. She isn't the type to throw herself recklessly into a casual affair. Once you've proven you're worth her while, she'll open up emotionally, and her depth may astonish you. She plays for keeps in love. She has a soft spot for animals, which often bring out the best in her because she opens to them emotionally.

Capricorn Man

He's well prepared for any journey he undertakes, and it doesn't matter whether the journey is physical, emotional, or spiritual. He doesn't like surprises. He shies away from getting involved in people's lives, and this detachment allows him to focus on his goals. As a boss, he can be dictatorial. As an employee, you won't find a harder worker.

He enjoys the company of vivacious women, perhaps because they make him feel lighter and less driven. Once he's committed, he tends to be monogamous. Life seems to improve for him as he ages because he has learned that discipline is not nearly as important as compassion.

Famous Capricorns
- Al Capone
- Cary Grant
- Catherine, Duchess of Cambridge
- Hamid Karzai
- James Earl Jones
- Janis Joplin
- Katie Couric
- Pat Benatar
- Tiger Woods
- Zooey Deschanel

Work

Capricorns excel in any profession that is structured, such as engineering, medicine, editing, politics, ceramics, building, architecture, and leatherwork. Their strong desire to succeed is colored by traditional values and a conservative approach.

Finances

Thriftiness is the hallmark for Capricorn finances. They build their finances the same way they build their careers: one penny at a time. They do seek status and the acquisition of material goods that reflect what they seek, so they may go through periods where they overspend.

Spirituality

Capricorns flourish within structured and firmly established parameters. Ritual speaks to them and inspires them. They bring the same serious efficiency to their involvement with spiritual beliefs as they do to other areas of their lives. In less evolved types, the expression of spiritual beliefs can manifest as dogma. In the highly evolved Capricorn, the soul clearly understands its purpose in life.

AQUARIUS

Water Bearer (January 20–February 18)

Element: Air
Quality: Fixed
Planetary Ruler: Uranus
Keywords: Altruism, individuality, freedom
Rules: Ankles, shins, and circulatory system; natural ruler of the eleventh house

Aquarians are original thinkers, often eccentric, who prize individuality and freedom above all else. The tribal mentality goes against their grain. They chafe at the restrictions placed upon them by society and seek to follow their own paths.

Aquarius is the sign of true genius because these people generally have the ability to think in unique ways. Once they make up their minds about something, nothing can convince them to change what they believe. This stubbornness is a double-edged sword; it can sustain them or destroy them. When the stubbornness manifests in small rebellions against the strictures of society, energy is wasted that could be put to better use.

Even though compassion is a hallmark of this Sun sign, Aquarians usually don't become emotionally involved with the causes they promote. Their compassion, while genuine, rises from the intellect rather than the heart. The Uranian influence confers a fascination with a broad spectrum of intellectual interests.

Aquarius Woman

Even when you know her well, she's hard to figure out because she's so often a paradox. She's patient but impatient; a nonconformist who conforms when it suits her; rebellious but peace-loving; stubborn and yet compliant when she wants to be.

Unconventional

In romance, the only "given" with this woman is that she's usually attracted to someone who is unusual or eccentric in some way. Even if the significant other appears to be conventional, he isn't. She's a good mother, and she allows her children the freedom to make their own decisions, revels in their accomplishments, and never lets them down.

She likes unusual people and has a variety of friends, both male and female. Economic status doesn't impress her, so her friends tend to come from a broad spectrum of backgrounds. She may dabble in tarot or astrology, have a passion for invention or writing, or may even be a budding filmmaker. Whatever her profession, it allows her latitude to do things her way.

Aquarius Man

He's often as inscrutable as his female counterpart and for the same reasons. He wants companionship, but not at the expense of his individuality. Even when he marries, he retains his independence to often irritating extremes. He might, for instance, fly off to some exotic place, leaving his wife or significant other to tend to his affairs at home.

The Aquarian man is fascinated by unusual people and places. Even though his attention is focused on the future, he may be interested in the mysteries of ancient cultures—how the pyramids were built, the true nature of Stonehenge, or the disappearance of the Anasazi. His travel to foreign cultures is often connected to these interests.

Aquarians are natural revolutionaries. If the restrictions placed on them are too confining, they rebel in a major way. But they need a place to which they can return; a sanctuary where they can refresh themselves. When the Aquarian man returns from his exotic journeys, he's eager to indulge himself in his family. As a parent, he may seem remote at times and perhaps somewhat undemonstrative, but his love for his offspring runs deep.

Famous Aquarians

- Bobby Brown
- Douglas MacArthur
- Hank Aaron
- Lana Turner
- Oprah Winfrey
- Paris Hilton
- Shakira
- Simon Pegg
- Yoko Ono

Work

Aquarians work best in avant garde fields: film, the arts, cutting-edge research in electronics, computers, or psychology. Many have raw psychic talent that can be developed into clairvoyance, remote viewing, and precognition, and most are very intuitive. The main element they seek in their work is freedom.

Finances

Aquarians are generous with their families and loved ones and that compassion extends to the larger scope of humanity as well. They stash money away, but the accumulation of wealth isn't the point; their freedom is.

Spirituality

The revolutionary nature of the sign definitely extends to spiritual issues. Even if an Aquarian is born into a family that follows the dictates of an organized religion, he or she probably won't stick to it. Aquarians insist on finding their own path and seek a broader spiritual spectrum that honors "the family of man."

PISCES

The Fish (February 19–March 20)

Element: Water
Quality: Mutable
Keywords: Compassion, mysticism
Planetary Ruler: Neptune
Rules: Externally, the feet and toes. Internally, Pisces rules the lymphatic system; natural ruler of the twelfth house

Pisceans need to explore their world through their emotions. They feel things so deeply that quite often they become a kind of psychic sponge, absorbing the emotions of people around them. Because of this, they should choose their friends and associates carefully.

People born under this sign usually have wonderful imaginations and great creative resources. They gravitate toward the arts, in general, and to theater and film, in particular. In the business world, they make powerful administrators and managers because they are so attuned to the thoughts of the people around them.

Swimming Away From Each Other

Pisces, represented by the fish swimming in opposite directions, can be ambivalent and indecisive simply because they're so impressionable. In highly evolved types, mystical tendencies are well developed, and the individuals possess deeply spiritual connections.

Pisces people need time alone so that they can detach from the emotions of people around them and center themselves. They are very impressionable. Without periodic solitude, it becomes increasingly difficult for them to sort out what they feel from what other people feel. They also tend to be moody because they feel the very height of joy and the utter depths of despair. Love and romance are essential for most Piscean individuals. These fulfill them emotionally, and Pisces generally flourish within stable relationships.

Pisces Woman

She's mysterious, with an air of complexity about her, as if she knows more than she's telling. Sometimes she even comes off as a snob, but it's just her regal composure showing. The lady is all feeling and possesses a quiet strength that hints at inner depths.

No Limits!

Don't ever be dogmatic with a Pisces woman! She refuses to be limited or restricted by anyone or anything that might inhibit her freedom of expression! This is reflected in her job, her home, and her relationship with her family and friends. This tendency may sometimes work against her, but she doesn't care. It's against her nature to be otherwise.

Even though she needs companionship, Pisces woman also craves her solitude. It's as essential to her well-being as harmony is to a Libra. When she doesn't have her time alone, she may be prone to alcohol or drug abuse. Properly channeled, her energy can produce astonishing works in art, literature, and music. In this instance, she becomes a mystical channel for the higher mind. As a mother, her psychic connection to her children allows her to understand what they're feeling even when they don't understand it themselves.

Pisces Man

His quiet strength and self-containment fascinate women. He's a good listener—the kind of man who gives you his full attention when you're talking. He's also a fine friend to people he trusts and is always there when his friends are in need. But, like his female counterpart, he's a sucker for a sob story; he can't stand seeing tragedies or heartbreaks in others.

In affairs of the heart, the Pisces man is a romantic, even if he doesn't want to admit it to himself. He likes candlelight dinners and intimate conversation. It may take him a while to fall head over heels in love, but, once he does, his emotions run deep and eternal.

The Pisces man may gravitate toward the arts or, because the sign rules the twelfth house, may work behind the scenes in some capacity. Whatever his path, he needs to learn to balance the demands of his inner life with his responsibilities in the external world.

Famous Pisces

- Alan Rickman
- Anne Bradstreet
- Chuck Norris
- Cindy Crawford
- Dr. Seuss
- Eva Mendez
- Li Na
- Quincy Jones
- Sharon Stone
- Tecumseh

Work

Pisces do well in anything that is behind the scenes. Due to their dreamy imaginations and mystical leanings, they excel in the arts, literature, and drama, or as monks, mystics, and even inventors.

Finances

Pisces is usually less concerned about money and material goods than he is about enjoying what he does to make a living. Can he transcend himself through his work? Does his tremendous compassion find expression through his work? If not, then he will undoubtedly change his work again and again, until he finds the job or profession that suits him.

Spirituality

Not all Pisces people are psychic, of course, or mystically inclined. Not all of them want to become monks or nuns, either. But most Pisces people are born with a deep intuitive sense, even if it's latent. And this sense is what connects them to a higher power. It may manifest within the parameters of organized religion—or it may veer into something less structured. Whatever form it takes, though, the intuitive side of Pisces constantly seeks expression.

CHAPTER 4

THE PLANETS

On a clear night, go outside and look up at the sky through a telescope. Look at the rings of Saturn, the red dust of Mars, and the stark landscape of the Moon. Suddenly, the stories about the Greek and Roman gods will leap to life for you.

As previously mentioned, planetary energy can be labeled as good and bad. Actually, this is misleading because planetary energy isn't positive or negative. Traditionally, Jupiter is the great benefic, the planet that blesses. Venus comes in a close second. The Sun, Moon, and Mercury line up after that. Saturn is the great malefic, the bad guy of the group whose lessons tend to be harsh. Saturn is followed in this negativity by Mars, Uranus, Neptune, and Pluto.

INNER AND OUTER PLANETS

Inner Selves, Outside World

Planets orbit the Sun at different speeds. The closer a planet is to the Sun, the faster it travels through its orbit. The Moon, for instance, travels through the zodiac in about twenty-eight days and spends two to three days in each sign. Mercury orbits the Sun in eighty-eight days. Pluto, which lies the farthest from the Sun, completes its orbit in 248 years. The faster moving planets—Moon, Mercury, Venus, Mars—are known as inner planets. Jupiter, Uranus, Neptune, and Pluto are known as outer planets.

The inner planets are considered to be personal because they relate to the development of our individual egos, our conscious selves. The outer planets relate to the outer world. Since the outer planets move so much more slowly through the zodiac, their pattern of influence is often felt by an entire generation of people.

The luminaries—Sun and Moon—have transpersonal qualities. The Sun represents not only our ego, but fundamental cosmic energy. The Moon, which concerns our most intimate emotions and urges, links us to what astrologer Robert Hand calls, "One's Ultimate Source."

Strengths and Weaknesses of the Planets

The strength or weakness of a planet depends on its sign, placement in the houses, aspects, and motion. A planet that occupies a sign it rules is *dignified*—Mercury in Gemini, for instance, or Venus in Libra.

When a planet is *exalted*, its drive and essential qualities are expressed more harmoniously. An example would be the Sun in Aries or the Moon in Taurus. Exalted planets are assigned specific degrees and are said to function smoothly within those degrees.

A planet is in the sign of *detriment* when it occupies the sign opposite that of its dignity. An example is Mercury in Sagittarius. Mercury is in detriment here because it rules Gemini, and Sagittarius is Gemini's polar opposite. In a detriment, the energy of the planet is considered to be at a disadvantage. When a planet lies in the sign opposite that of its exaltation, it's said to be *in fall*. A Moon in Scorpio is in fall because the Moon is exalted in Taurus. Its energy is watered down.

Ruling the Ascendant

One of the most important planets in a chart is the one that rules the ascendant (or rising sign). This planet is usually, but not always, considered the ruler of the chart. A Libra rising, for example, means that Venus is the chart ruler because Venus rules Libra.

Mutual reception occurs when two planets are placed in each other's sign of dignity. The Sun and the Moon, for instance, are in mutual reception if the Sun is in Cancer or Taurus, and the Moon is in Leo or Aries. This happens because the Sun rules Leo and is exalted in Aries, and the Moon rules Cancer and is exalted in Taurus. When a planet is placed in its natural house of the horoscope (Mercury in the third house, for instance), it's *accidentally dignified* and strengthened.

Retrograde and Direct Motion

The movement of the planets through the night sky was what first attracted the attention of the ancient Greeks to them (the Greek word *planetes* means "travelers"). However, the Greeks soon realized that this motion, although regular, had some peculiarities.

Planetary motion is either direct (D), retrograde (R), or stationary (S). In reality, all planetary motion is direct but relative motion isn't. The

Sun and the Moon can never turn retrograde, but all the other planets do. A retrograde planet is one that appears to move backward in the zodiac, but this backward motion is actually an optical illusion caused by the fact that the Earth is also moving. Imagine being in a train as another train speeds past you. You feel as if you're moving backward, when in actuality, you're only moving more slowly than the other train. Retrograde motion doesn't change the fundamental essence of a planet; it merely means that the expression of its energy is altered somewhat.

Retrograde motion of the planets has specific meanings in astrological lore.

Beware Mercury Retrograde

During a Mercury retrograde, communications tend to get fouled up and travel plans are disrupted. Back up your computer files beforehand! Don't sign new contracts! This is an important time to revisit the past and work on old projects. It's not a time to start something new.

During a Jupiter retrograde, the beneficial aspects of the planet are turned down somewhat. Some astrologers contend that if there are three or more retrograde planets in a chart, certain past-life patterns may prevail in the present life. But even if it is true, our point of power lies in the present, in this life; this moment.

During a retrograde, the nature of that planet is forced inward, where it creates tension and stress. The outlet for this tension is usually worked out in relationships with others.

Planets in direct motion have more influence than retrograde planets. Stationary planets, those that are about to turn direct or retrograde, have greater influence in a chart than either retrograde or direct moving planets. This is due to the concentrated energy of the planet.

MERCURY

The Messenger Planet

Mercury is the messenger; it speaks in terms of logic and reasoning. The left brain is its vehicle. Mercury represents how we think and how we communicate those thoughts. Mercury also is concerned with travel of the routine variety—work commutes, trips across town, weekend excursions, or a visit with siblings and neighbors—rather than long distance travel.

Searching for the New

Restlessness is inherent to Mercury because it craves movement, newness, and the bright hope of undiscovered terrains. Mercury often tackles something new before the old has been assimilated. On a higher level, Mercury seeks to understand the deeper connections between the physical universe and the divine.

Mercury orbits the Sun in about eighty-eight days. It goes retrograde every few months, and, during that time, communications and travel plans go haywire. Your computer may go down, lightning may blow out your electricity, or you may spend hours in an airport waiting for a flight that is ultimately canceled. It's best not to sign contracts when Mercury is retrograde.

Mercury rules any profession dealing with writing, teaching, speaking, books, and publications. Mercury is the natural ruler of the third and sixth houses and governs Gemini and Virgo. It rules arms, hands, shoulders, lungs, the solar plexus, abdomen, intestines, the thymus gland, and the nervous and respiratory systems.

VENUS

Planet of Love

Venus governs our ability to attract compatible people, to create close personal relationships, and to form business partnerships. It expresses how we relate to other people one-on-one and how we express ourselves in marriage and in romantic relationships.

Venus the Goddess

Venus, called Aphrodite by the Greeks, is the goddess of love and beauty, sex and desire. She was an indirect cause of the Trojan War (Paris, prince of Troy, awarded her the golden apple in return for her offer of Helen as his beloved), and her son, Aeneas, became the founder of the Roman people. One of the most important temples dedicated to her was on the Capitoline Hill in ancient Rome.

Venus is also associated with the arts and the aesthetic sense, and it has enormous influence on our tastes in art, music, and literature. The sign and placement of Venus, as well as its aspects, determine our refinement—or lack of it. This planet also has some bearing on material resources, earning capacity, and spending habits. A strong Venus enhances these things; a poorly placed or badly aspected Venus generates laziness, self-indulgence, extravagance, and discord in partnerships.

Venus orbits the Sun in 255 days. It spends about four weeks in a sign when moving directly and is retrograde for about six weeks. It rules all professions having to do with the arts and music. Its natural houses are the second and the seventh, and it governs Taurus and Libra. It rules the neck, throat, thyroid gland, kidneys, ovaries, veins, and circulation of the venous blood. It shares rulership with the Moon over the female sex organs.

MARS

Energy and Aggression

Mars dictates our survival energy and the shape that energy assumes as we define ourselves in terms of the larger world. It represents the individualization process, particularly in a romantic relationship. A weak Mars placement in a woman's chart may make her too passive and submissive in a love relationship, especially if her significant other has a strongly placed Mars.

Mars rules athletes and competitions. The Mars individual seeks to take himself to the limit—and then surpass that limit. He refuses to compromise his integrity by following another's agenda. He doesn't compare himself to other people and doesn't want to dominate or be dominated. He simply wants to be free to follow his own path, whatever it is.

Is Mars "Good" or "Bad"?

Actually, Mars's energy can be either constructive or destructive; it depends on how it's channeled. Rage, violence, and brutality can manifest if the energy is poorly channeled. When properly channeled, Mars's energy manifests as stamina and achievement.

Mars orbits the Sun in 687 days. It spends six to eight weeks in a sign. When retrograde, it sits in a sign for two and a half months. As the god of war, Mars governs the military, rules Aries, and is co-ruler of Scorpio. Its natural houses are the first and the eighth. It rules the head, general musculature of the body, the sex organs in general—the male sex organs in particular—the anus, red corpuscles, and hemoglobin.

JUPITER

Your Luck, Your Higher Mind

Tradition views Jupiter as associated with luck, success, achievement, and prosperity. But it can also indicate excess, laziness, and other less desirable traits. However, Jupiter's energies are usually constructive.

King of the Gods

Jupiter (or Zeus, as he was called in Greece) ruled all the other gods, a task he found difficult since they were a quarrelsome lot. Jupiter is associated with thunder, and statues of him often show him holding a thunderbolt, with which he dispatches those who challenge him.

This planet's energy allows us to reach out beyond ourselves and expand our consciousness. It confers a love of travel and a need to explore religious and philosophical ideas. Jupiter also allows us to integrate ourselves into the larger social order—church or religion, community, and corporation. Since Jupiter rules the abstract mind, it describes our intellectual and spiritual interests in the most profound sense.

Jupiter takes about twelve years to traverse the zodiac and averages a year in every sign. It governs publishing, the travel profession, universities and other institutions of higher learning, and traditional organized religions. Its natural houses are the ninth and the twelfth. It rules Sagittarius. Jupiter oversees the blood in general, arteries, hips, thighs, and feet (with Neptune).

SATURN

Your Responsibilities

Saturn has long been known as a maleficent influence. While it's true that its lessons are sometimes harsh, it also provides structure and foundation, and teaches us through experience what we need in order to grow. It shows us the limitations we have and teaches us the rules of the game in this physical reality.

Even if you don't believe in reincarnation, there's ample evidence that Saturn holds a key to what the soul intends to accomplish in this life. People with a well-placed or well-aspected Saturn tend to have a practical, prudent outlook.

Unsettling Aspects

When poorly aspected, Saturn creates rigid belief systems, restricts growth, and closes us off to other possibilities. A delicate balance must be attained with Saturn influences. Even though it pushes us to understand and work with limitations, it can also cause us to settle for too little, or to deny our creative expression because we don't want to see what is really possible.

As one of the outer, slowly moving planets, Saturn takes twenty-nine and a half years to cross the zodiac. Its natural houses are the tenth and the eleventh. Saturn rules Capricorn. This planet governs the bones and joints, skin, and teeth.

URANUS

Your Individuality

Uranian disruptions appear to bring unpleasant and unexpected surprises. In reality, these disruptions liberate us, revolutionize the way we do things, and blow out the old so that the new can flow in.

The Sky God

Uranus, or Ouranos, was the name given by the Greeks to the god of the sky (the Roman equivalent was Caelus). Uranus mated with the Earth (Gaia) and gave birth to a series of monstrous children: the titans, giants, and cyclopes. Uranus imprisoned them in the Earth, but one, Cronos, broke free and castrated his father. From the blood that dripped into the sea was born Venus.

Uranus, like the other outer planets, remains in a sign for so long that its effect is widely felt. In the twenty-first century, this planet's influence is visible in the breakdown of old paradigms of belief within most of the large structures we have taken for granted: healthcare, medicine, science, religion, lifestyle, education, and social programs. We are in the early decades of a new century with old structures crumbling around us. But in the shadows, the new paradigms are forming, bubbling with vitality, gathering momentum. This is all part of the Uranian influence.

In a horoscope, Uranus dictates the areas of our life in which these disruptions occur and how we utilize this energy. Do we feel it? Think about it? Seize it? Pull it deep within us so that this becomes rooted in who we are? Are we so afraid of it that we deny it? Uranus also indicates the areas in which we are most inventive, creative, and original.

This planet takes eighty-four years to go through the zodiac. Its natural house is the eleventh, and it rules Aquarius. Traditionally, before the discovery of Uranus in 1781, Saturn ruled this sign. But Saturn's rigidity just doesn't fit Aquarius. It governs electricity, inventions, the avant garde, everything that is unpredictable or sudden.

NEPTUNE

Your Visionary Self

This planet stimulates the imagination, dreams, psychic experiences, artistic inspiration, flashes or insight, mystical tendencies. On the downside, it deals with all forms of escapism—drug and alcohol addiction, as well as delusion (and false idealism).

Neptune, like Uranus, overpowers Saturn's rigidity. Where Uranus disrupts the rigidity, Neptune simply negates it. This planet is considered the higher octave of Venus, and when it operates in the chart of an evolved soul, its music is extraordinary.

Neptune's Energy

Most of us experience Neptune through synchronous events and flashes of insight that seem to come out of nowhere. Perhaps we lose ourselves in the illusions we've created. The best way to appreciate Neptune's energy is while we are in quiet contemplation—meditation, yoga, listening to music, writing, or through some activity that involves water.

Neptune takes 165 years to cross the zodiac and spends about fourteen years in each sign. The twelfth house is its natural domain and it rules Pisces. It governs shipping, dance, film, and the arts in general, and is associated with mediums, clairvoyants, psychic healers, and both white and black magic.

PLUTO

Transforming and Regenerating

Although it sometimes works in subtle ways, the influence of Pluto in our lives is far-reaching and transformational. Its two extremes are best symbolized by Hitler and Gandhi, each man possessed of a vision that he manifested in physical reality. Both had a mission, a sense of destiny, but one caused massive destruction and the other elevated mass consciousness.

In our personal lives, Pluto's influence works in the same way. Pluto tears down our habits and belief systems, the very structures that Saturn has helped us build, thus forcing us to transcend the ruin—or to smother in the debris.

King of the Underworld

Pluto (Hades to the Greeks) was the ruler of the vast underground realm of the dead. Pluto (or Hades) carried off Persephone, daughter of the goddess Demeter, to be his bride. Her mother mourned for her, and the world became cold and barren. Finally Pluto relented and allowed the girl to rejoin her mother but only for six months of the year. So for six months, the world is warm and full of light and life, and then, when Persephone returns to her shadowy world, the upper lands are gripped by winter.

A Pluto placement in Sagittarius, in the ninth house of philosophy and spiritual beliefs, would mean you evolve through expansion of your beliefs in these areas. But before you do, Pluto will destroy your old beliefs, collapsing them like a house of cards.

Ruler of the Occult

Pluto, the higher octave of Mars, governs various types of occult practices: black magic, levitation, witchcraft, and reincarnation. On a personal level in a horoscope, Pluto's influence is most powerful when it occupies a prominent place or rules the chart.

Pluto, discovered in 1930, is the most distant planet from the Sun. It exists at the very edge of our solar system—its light is so dim that Pluto seems almost etheric. It takes 248 years to complete a circuit of the zodiac. Popular astrological theory says that Pluto, like Uranus and Neptune, wasn't discovered until humanity had evolved to be able to understand its energy.

Planet or Not-a-Planet?

In 2005, astronomers reclassified Pluto as a "dwarf planet," since several other bodies in its vicinity were found to be more massive. However, the public has resented this, and the classification of Pluto as not-a-planet continues to be discussed.

Through Pluto, we tap into that which is larger than our individual selves. We tap into the collective mind in all its hypnotizing horror and magnificent beauty.

Since Pluto's discovery, its influence has been observed in only Cancer, Leo, Virgo, Libra, and Scorpio. In late fall 1995, Pluto slipped into Sagittarius. The transformation under this influence is apt to be enormous and far-reaching, completing the collapse of old paradigms and belief systems.

SUN AND MOON
Ego and Emotions

The Sun is the very essence and energy of life—the manifestation of will, power, and desire. It represents the ego, individuality, the yang principle, and is the thrust that allows us to meet challenges and expand our lives. The Sun represents a person's creative abilities and the general state of his or her physical health.

The Sun embraces the fatherhood principle and in a chart, symbolizes a person's natural father and a woman's husband. As natural ruler of the fifth house, it rules children in general and the firstborn in particular. Leo is ruled by the Sun—fire.

The Sun spends about a month in each sign, with a mean daily motion of 59'8". It rules occupations of power and authority—royalty and religious and spiritual rulers. Its natural house is the fifth, and it governs the sign of Leo. It rules the heart, back, spine, and spinal cord.

Leadership

Since the Sun also symbolizes authority and power, a strongly placed Sun confers leadership ability. A Sun that is badly aspected or weakly placed lessens the natural vitality and may make it difficult for the person to express basic drives and desires.

The Moon

The Moon is your emotions—the inner you. It's intuition, the mother, the yin principle. Coupled with the Sun and the Ascendant, the Moon is one of the vital parts of a chart. It describes our emotional reactions to situations, how emotions flow through us, motivating and compelling us—or limiting us and holding us back.

The Moon symbolizes a person's mother and the relationship between mother and child. In a man's chart, the Moon represents his wife; in a woman's chart, it describes pregnancies, childbirth, and intuition. Symbolically, the Moon represents our capacity to become part of the whole rather than attempting to master the parts. It asks that we become whatever it is that we seek.

How the Moon Defines You

Your Moon represents your emotions—how you instinctively respond to things. For example, if someone says something nasty to you, how do you react? If your Sun sign is Leo, but your Moon sign is Gemini, chances are that you'll react, immediately, as a Gemini would. After the tension is gone, you'll go back to being your regal, Leo self.

As Earth's satellite, the Moon moves more swiftly than any of the planets, completing a circuit of the zodiac in less than twenty-eight days. It rules activities and professions dealing with children and those that concern the sea. Its natural house is the fourth and it governs the sign of Cancer. The stomach, breasts, mammary glands, womb, conception, and the body fluids in general are ruled by the Moon.

LUNAR-BASED ASTROLOGY
The Moon Foretells

Some astrologers practice a form of the art in which the Moon plays the central role. To lunar astrologers, the Moon has eight phases:

1. New Moon
2. Waxing Crescent
3. Waxing Quarter
4. Gibbous
5. Full
6. Disseminating
7. Waning Quarter
8. Balsamic

You can find a number of websites that will provide you with an astrological lunar calendar. One of the best is *www.moonconnection.com.*

Lunar Conjunctions

If, on your zodiac chart, a planet is within ten degrees of the Moon glyph, the planet is in conjunction with your Moon. Consult the list below:

- The Sun rules the Leo Moon
- The Moon rules the Cancer Moon
- Mercury rules the Gemini Moon and the Virgo Moon
- Venus rules the Taurus Moon and the Libra Moon
- Mars rules the Aries Moon
- Jupiter rules the Sagittarius Moon
- Saturn rules the Capricorn Moon
- Uranus rules the Aquarius Moon

- Neptune rules the Pisces Moon
- Pluto rules the Scorpio Moon

If your Moon conjuncts with a planet, the planet will exert an influence on you—greater or less, depending on the degree of conjunction. We don't have space here to consider in detail all the phases of the Moon in the various houses. Here's a brief summary of the Moon's phases and what they mean.

New Moon

A time of beginnings, when the Moon is hidden from our sight but its potential is there, ready to burst forth. To be born under a New Moon can give someone a trusting, childlike persona. It can also make that person wounded or wild. This is a powerful phase of the Moon, especially when it is in conjunction with the Sun.

Waxing Crescent Moon

With this phase, the Moon swings into movement. It sets us on our path and gives us direction. Those born under a Crescent Moon will take risks but will think about the consequences. They're attempting to plot out the road ahead rather than suddenly change directions. It also takes us out of our comfort zone and sets us to sail strange seas.

Waxing Quarter Moon

The Waxing Quarter Moon is a place of decisions—sometimes very difficult ones. Often people born under this sign struggle with having to take responsibility for their lives. In fact, though, the challenges this phase presents can be overcome and can strengthen character.

Gibbous Moon

This phase is described by lunar astrologer Raven Kaldera as "a pit created by [the soul's] own response to hard choices." Now, though, the struggle to resolve the crisis is directed and energetic rather than a helpless thrashing around. Those born under this sign will do what is necessary to achieve their goals.

Full Moon

This is a time of fulfillment, when the work of the previous four phases comes to fruition. Although it can resolve many issues, it is not the end. Yet people born under a Full Moon are generally happy with themselves and infused with energy.

Disseminating Moon

A shadow creeping across the face of the Moon marks an awakening from the contentment of the Full Moon. There is some insecurity, and those born under this phase will often call upon others to help them achieve their ends. At the same time, this means they are good at cooperation.

Waning Quarter Moon

This phase represents a new crisis, a time of tension and conflict. This Moon is about external conflict rather than internal, about rejection of your goals and dreams by forces outside you. If you were born under this Moon, you may feel that the world is conspiring to thwart you. However, by working with others you can still triumph.

Balsamic Moon

The Moon is preparing to enter the New Moon phase and be reborn, so it's not surprising that this last phase is one of sinking slowly into peace. Everything is calmer, and those who are born under this Moon may be inclined to say, "Whatever!" when faced with a challenge or something different. They are more at peace with themselves and thus more accepting.

CHAPTER 5

PLANETS AND THE SIGNS

So far we've considered the planets by themselves. But on an astrological birth chart, the planets exist in relationship to the signs. The sign a planet occupies describes how that particular energy permeates your personality and influences your life. If you have eight out of ten planets in Fire signs, then you probably have abundant energy and a fierce temper, and tend to initiate action. If you have mostly Air planets, your approach to life comes from a mental standpoint—rationalizing and thinking before acting.

THE MOON AND THE SIGNS

The Power of Instinct

The Moon expresses your emotions, the inner you, that which makes you feel secure.

Aries Moon. Your emotions are all fire. You're passionate, impulsive, and headstrong. Your own actions ground you. You take pride in your ability to make decisions and to get things moving.

Taurus Moon (exalted). You don't like to argue. You need time alone and thrive in your private spaces, whatever they might be. Your emotional well-being depends on the harmony of your emotional attachments.

Gemini Moon. You thrive on change and variety. Your emotions fluctuate and sometimes you think too much, analyzing what you feel and why. Your capacity for adaptability, however, sees you through.

Cancer Moon (dignified). You have strong family ties and feel a need to nurture or nourish others. At times, you're very psychic; other times you're merely moody. You don't like emotional confrontations and seek to sidestep them.

Leo Moon. Your emotions are often dramatic. You feel cheerful and optimistic about life in general. You enjoy the limelight and being recognized for what you do and who you are.

Virgo Moon. You tend to be somewhat reticent about what you feel. You feel happy when you're of service to others and take pride in your meticulous attention to details. You can be overly critical of your personal relationships and of yourself.

Libra Moon. Discord makes you feel anxious. You thrive on harmony in your personal environment and need compatible relationships for your emotional well-being. You go out of your way to avoid confrontations.

Scorpio Moon (in fall). Your emotions and passions run deep. You feel a profound loyalty to your family and the people you love. You possess great strength and are able to draw on it during times of crisis. You rarely forget it when someone has slighted you.

Sagittarius Moon. You need emotional freedom and independence. You need your own space so you can explore everything that fascinates you—foreign cultures, inner worlds, or the distant future. None of this means that you love your significant other any less; you simply need your freedom.

Respect!

A person with a Sagittarius Moon needs to be respected. He may have a problem with authority—especially at work. It's very difficult for him to bow down to a boss or even a coworker if he doesn't feel the other person is justified in his higher standing.

Capricorn Moon (detriment). You need structure of some sort to feel emotionally secure. You aren't as emotionally aloof as some people think; you just don't wear your heart on your sleeve.

Aquarius Moon. Your compassion extends to humanity. Your home life is important to you, but it's definitely not traditional. You don't recognize boundaries or limitations of any sort.

Pisces Moon. Sometimes, you're a psychic sponge; you soak up emotions from others and may even manifest those emotions. Your compassion sometimes makes you gullible and impractical. Your artistic sensibilities are strong.

MERCURY AND THE SIGNS

Communicating Your Ideas

The sign Mercury describes how you express your mental habits and how you gather information. This sign also shows how you study and how you communicate your ideas in life.

Mercury in Aries. You have a quick, decisive mind that makes snap judgments. You're often argumentative but intuitive about the dynamics of relationships.

Mercury in Taurus. Yours is a practical, determined mind with strong likes and dislikes. You have intuition about the practical aspects of relationships and love beautiful, flowing language.

Mercury in Gemini (dignified). Marked by a quick, inventive mind, you're up-to-date on current events and have shrewd powers of observation. You have an adaptable, versatile intellect, ease with language, and intuition about the structure of relationships.

Mercury in Cancer. Your sensitive, imaginative mind also has excellent powers of retention. However, your opinions change quickly. You're interested in psychic matters and may have psychic abilities as well. You're intuitive about the inner connections in relationships.

Mercury in Leo (in fall). Great willpower and lofty ideals characterize you. Your intellect can be self-centered, but intuitive. Your intellectual efforts often carry your personal unique style.

Mercury in Virgo. You have facility with language and as a linguist. Mentally, you display great attention to detail, which can collapse into criticism and nitpicky tendencies. There's a deep interest in mystery, the occult, and magic, and you have excellent intellect overall.

Mercury in Libra. Yours is a refined intellect, capable of broad scope. You are excellent at balancing issues and intuitive about the innate balance in relationships. This is good placement for any artistic pursuit, particularly music.

Libra and Beauty

Libra is particularly drawn to beauty; he has an easier time chatting it up with someone he finds attractive. A person with Mercury in Libra will get along well with someone who has his Sun in Libra.

Mercury in Scorpio. You have a suspicious but deeply intuitive intellect capable of probing beneath the obvious. You also have a mental need to perceive the hidden order of things, to pierce that order, and pull out the truth. You can be sarcastic and wry in communication.

Mercury in Sagittarius (detriment). You're idealistic and intellectually versatile. Your personal opinions sometimes are inflated and become principles rather than just personal opinions.

Mercury in Capricorn. You're characterized by mental discipline and organizational ability. Your intellect is sometimes structured in a way that inhibits imagination. You experience much serious and thoughtful contemplation.

Mercury in Aquarius (exalted). Your intellect is detached from emotion and endlessly inventive. Your mental interests tend to be progressive, unusual, and often eccentric. You exhibit interest in the occult and science.

Mercury in Pisces (detriment). Your psychic impressions are often so pronounced that reasoning ability is clouded. Great imagination and creativity are indicated and much information is culled through intuitive means.

VENUS AND THE SIGNS

Love in the Houses

The sign in which Venus falls describes your artistic nature and what you are like as a romantic partner, spouse, or friend. Venus's sign also indicates financial and spending habits.

Venus in Aries (detriment). You exhibit aggressive social interaction and passion in romantic relationships. You form impetuous, impulsive ties and are self-centered in love. For you, marriage may happen early or in haste.

Venus in Taurus (dignified). Heightened artistic expression. You attract money and material resources easily. You form deeply emotional love attachments. You have strong financial drive.

Venus in Gemini. You're a good conversationalist, you're popular, and you enjoy reading and travel. You also have a tendency for short-lived relationships, which can occur simultaneously. You're a spendthrift who earns money from a variety of sources.

Venus in Cancer. Home and marriage are important and offer you a sense of security. Family ties are strong. You spend money on home and family, but also squirrel it away in savings. You benefit through houses, land, and wide, open spaces. Being near water gives you a sense of tranquility.

Venus in Cancer a Paradox?

Although Venus in Cancer can be clingy and needs security in love, there can be a tendency for secret love affairs. And settling down—though that is what Cancer wants most—is his greatest fear. Venus in Cancer also may have a deep interest in the occult.

Venus in Leo. You're ardent in relationships and have a gregarious nature. You may have a pronounced talent in one of the arts. You like to entertain and gamble and have a strong attraction to the opposite sex. You gain through investments and speculation.

Venus in Virgo (in fall). Secret romances, disappointment through love, and possibly more than one marriage may befall you. You're too analytical and criticize romantic relationships and emotions. You're a perfectionist about artistic self-expression.

Venus in Libra (dignified). You have a kind, sympathetic nature and love the arts, music, and drama. You have a happy marriage with talented children. You earn money through areas that Venus rules and seek harmony in all your relationships.

Venus in Scorpio (detriment). You have a passionate nature and dominant sex drive. For you, marriage can be delayed and relationships are often stormy. You gain financially through inheritances, taxes, insurance, and the occult.

Venus in Sagittarius. You have a generous nature and ardent emotions in love. If your relationships threaten your personal freedom, however, your emotions cool rapidly. Love of arts, travel, and animals, with a particular fondness for horses, characterizes you.

Venus in Capricorn. You exercise restraint in emotions and experience some disappointment in love and romance. Marriage is usually for practical reasons and may be to someone older and more established financially. Your emphasis is on acquiring financial and material assets.

Venus in Aquarius. You have friends from all walks of life and strange, unexpected experiences in romance and friendships. You have a need for intellectual stimulation in romantic partnerships and exhibit erratic financial habits. You gain through friends, partnerships, and speculations.

Stay Faithful . . . Or Not

It's tough to keep Venus in Aquarius faithful. They like to try new things and experience new people. They love the drama. They may even have an affair just to get attention from a partner who's not spending enough time with them.

Venus in Pisces (exalted). You have a charitable, compassionate nature. More than one marriage is likely for you. Romantic love and emotional attachments are necessary to your well-being. You exhibit great sensitivity to others and psychic abilities are likely.

MARS AND THE SIGNS

Stamina and Sex Drive

The planet Mars describes how you use energy in life. It also indicates your physical stamina and the nature of your sexual drive with a partner. Mars is also the expression of your desire for personal achievement.

Mars in Aries (dignified). You go after what you want. Your strong sex drive sometimes manifests selfishly, with little regard for the partner. Initiative and drive are highly developed, but due to haste and impulsiveness, there can be a tendency not to finish what you've started.

Mars in Taurus (detriment). You're not easily thwarted or discouraged by obstacles. Your sheer determination and strength of will are well-developed, but may not be used to the fullest. You prefer purposeful, practical action to achieve what you want. Your sexual nature is sensual, but can be somewhat passive.

Mars in Gemini. Energy is expressed mentally, through a keen intellect and versatile mind. You tend to take on too many projects that scatter your energy. Your mental restlessness needs a creative outlet or otherwise you become argumentative.

Mars in Cancer (in fall). You take everything personally and find it difficult to be objective about issues that are important to you. Your sex drive is overshadowed by deep emotional needs.

Mars in Leo. Passion rules the expression of your energy. You possess good leadership ability, a fearless nature, and a determined will. You need to be appreciated for who you are and as a lover. Mechanical or musical skill may be indicated.

Mars in Virgo. You express your energy through efficient, practical pursuits. You're an excellent worker, particularly if the work involves attention to detail. You apply your will quietly, with subtlety. Your sexual drive may be somewhat repressed, with the energy channeled into work.

Mars in Libra (detriment). You benefit through partnerships and express your energy best with and through other people. This placement of Mars is good for a lawyer or surgeon. You're a romantic when it comes to sex.

Mars in Scorpio (dignified). Your drive and ambition are legendary. It's difficult and sometimes downright impossible for you to compromise. Secrecy surrounds your personal projects. You make a formidable enemy and ally.

Mars in Sagittarius. You have the courage to act on your convictions. This is good placement for orators, crusaders, evangelists, and New Age leaders. You have a passionate sex drive but are often impulsive and noncommittal in your relationships.

Mars in Capricorn (exalted). Your worldly ambitions may take you into public life. You're able to plan well and to work practically to realize your ambitions and goals. You tend to keep a tight rein on your sex drive and may get involved with people who are older than you are.

Mars in Aquarius. Your unique approach may brand you as an eccentric. You act independently to achieve your goals, which are often directed toward humanity in general. Your approach to sex is apt to be rather unemotional.

Mars in Pisces. You're either inconsistent in what you seek to achieve or you're able to pull together various facets of a project and make them work. Sex drive is intimately linked with emotions. You try to avoid conflict and confrontations.

JUPITER AND THE SIGNS

Moral and Spiritual Beliefs

The sign in which Jupiter falls describes how you seek to expand your understanding of life, the benefits you receive, and how you express your intellectual, moral, religious, or spiritual beliefs. Jupiter is the farthest of the outer planets, which relate to the larger social world.

Jupiter in Aries. You're zealous in your beliefs and are convinced you're right, whether you are or not. You expand your life through personal initiative, seizing opportunities when you see them or creating your own opportunities. You gain through travel, children, law, and friends.

Jupiter in Taurus. Your approach is practical. You seek to apply spiritual and philosophical principles to daily life. You gain through children and marriage and greatly love your home. Your generosity to others is a result of their need rather than your sympathy.

Jupiter in Gemini (detriment). The hunger for knowledge and the acquisition of information and facts expand your world. Your travels are usually connected to your quest for understanding larger philosophical or spiritual issues. Benefits come through publishing, education, and psychic investigations.

Jupiter in Cancer (exalted). You hold onto the spiritual and moral ideals of your parents and pass these teachings down to your own children. Your spiritual beliefs are expanded through your compassion for others. Benefits come through your parents, family, and home-related matters.

Jupiter in Leo. Your beliefs are dramatized; you act on them, promote them, live them. In doing so, you attract others who help expand your world. Your exuberance, however, may be interpreted by some as outright pride. You gain through overseas trips that are connected with education, sports, or diplomatic issues.

Jupiter in Virgo (detriment). Through your work ethic and service to others, you expand your philosophical and spiritual horizons. You bring a critical and analytical mind to your profession. You gain through relationships with employees, and business and professional pursuits.

Jupiter in Libra. You expand your life through your associations with other people and through marriage and partnerships in general. You benefit from the opposite sex. Your sense of fair play and justice are well developed.

Jupiter in Scorpio. You expand through your relentless search to understand your beliefs and how they relate to the nature of reality. Your willpower and determination are your greatest assets in overcoming any obstacles in your search. You gain through inheritances, psychic investigation, and any areas that Scorpio governs.

Jupiter in Sagittarius (dignified). Your deep need to understand spiritual and philosophical issues broadens your life. Travel, foreign travel in particular, and education benefit your search. This is a lucky placement for Jupiter and usually denotes success in the area described by the house in which it falls. You benefit through all things associated with Sagittarius.

Jupiter in Capricorn (in fall). Your philosophical and spiritual expansion happens mostly through your own efforts. You seek to accumulate wealth, have a great appreciation for money, and tend to be guarded in your financial generosity. You gain through your father, employers, and commercial affairs.

Jupiter in Aquarius. Your progressive views and willingness to explore all kinds of spiritual beliefs expand who and what you are. Your tolerance for other people's beliefs deepens your understanding of beliefs that differ from yours. Benefits come to you through your profession and through group associations.

Jupiter in Pisces (dignified). Your compassion, emotional sensitivity, and imagination expand your philosophical and spiritual foundations. Benefits come through psychic and occult investigations and anything to do with behind-the-scenes activities. Look toward the sign and house placement of the aspects to Pisces to find out what pushes your buttons.

SATURN AND THE SIGNS

The Karmic Planet

The restrictions and structure inherent to Saturn are expressed through the sign it occupies. The sign shows how you handle obstacles in your life, deal with authority, and how you cope with serious issues. Actually, Saturn is thought to be the "karmic" planet of the zodiac. The house placement is personally significant because it shows what area of your life is affected.

Saturn in Aries (in fall). Circumstances force you to develop patience and initiative. Your impulsiveness needs to be mitigated, otherwise setbacks occur. With this position, there's a capacity for great resourcefulness which, constructively channeled, can lead to innovative creations. On the negative side, you can be self-centered and defensive.

Saturn in Taurus. You feel a deep need for financial and material security. But material comfort is earned only through hard work, discipline, and perseverance. As a result, you need to cultivate reliability and persistence in your chosen profession.

Stubborn Saturn

The downside to this placement—Saturn in Taurus—is that there can be a tendency for stubbornness in all issues of life: being right all the time. There may also be an excessive preoccupation with material affairs and goods for this person.

Saturn in Gemini. Discipline and structure are expressed mentally through your systematic and logical mind. Problems must be thought through carefully and worked out in detail; otherwise, difficulties multiply. You seek practical solutions.

Saturn in Cancer (detriment). Your crab-like tenacity sees you through most obstacles and difficulties. You choose a course, which may not always be the best, that doesn't threaten your emotional and financial security. Psychic and intuitive resources are sometimes stifled.

Saturn in Leo (detriment). Your ego and need for recognition can be your worst enemies. If you try to solve your difficulties in a self-centered way, you only compound the problem. Cooperative ventures and consideration of mutual needs work wonders for this placement.

Saturn in Virgo. You're such a perfectionist, you tend to get bogged down in details. You need to separate the essential from the inconsequential. An intuitive approach to obstacles and challenges is an enormous help with this placement.

Saturn in Libra (exalted). You overcome obstacles and difficulties by cooperation and a willingness to work with others. The best way to achieve your goals is in partnership with others. You have the opportunity to develop an acute sense of balance and timing with this placement.

Saturn in Scorpio. You handle your difficulties in an intense, secretive manner, which increases the suspicion of those around you. By being more open and up front about what you're doing, you're able to overcome obstacles. Work to discipline your intuition; it can be an infallible guide.

Saturn in Sagittarius. You need to loosen up. Any kind of rigid approach only increases your problems and difficulties. Your best bet is to structure your life by incorporating your ideals into a practical, daily life. Your intense intellectual pride makes you vulnerable to criticism by peers.

Saturn in Capricorn (dignified). No matter what challenges you face, your ambition conquers them. You respect the power structures that you see. For you, life itself is serious business. Don't get locked into rigid belief systems; remain flexible.

Saturn in Aquarius (dignified). Your emotional detachment and objectivity allow you to meet challenges head-on. Your innovative and unique approach to problems is best funneled through a quiet, practical application to daily life. Your peers help you to learn discipline.

Saturn in Pisces. Instead of letting yourself become trapped in memories of the past, use past triumphs as a springboard to the future. Your psychic ability is a doorway to higher spiritual truths but must be grounded in some way, perhaps through meditation or yoga.

URANUS AND THE SIGNS

Your Individuality

Uranus remains in the same sign for about seven years; the sign indicates the ways in which your urge for freedom and individuality are manifested. The house placement is more significant on a personal level because it shows what area of your life is impacted.

Uranus in Aries. Your spirit of adventure is quite pronounced and prompts you to seek freedom at almost any price. You're blunt, outspoken, and can have a fiery temper. You need to develop more consideration for others.

Uranus in Taurus (in fall). You're looking for new, practical ideas concerning the use of money and financial resources, so that the old way of doing things can be reformed. You have tremendous determination and purpose. Carried to extremes, your stubbornness can impede your progress.

Uranus in Gemini. Your ingenuity and intuitive brilliance impel you to pioneer new concepts in the areas where you're passionate. But your deep restlessness can make it difficult for you to follow an idea through to completion. Self-discipline will help you to bring your ideas to fruition.

Uranus in Cancer. You pursue freedom through emotional expression and seek independence from parental authority that restricts you in some way. Your own home is unusual, either in decor or in the way you run your domestic life. There can be great psychic sensitivity with this placement, which may manifest as occult or spiritual activities in the home.

Uranus in Leo (detriment). Your route to freedom and independence can touch several different areas: love and romance, leadership, and the arts. Sometimes it can encompass all three. Regardless of how it manifests, you chafe at existing standards, so you create your own.

Watch Out for Egos!

With Uranus in Leo, the risk of egotism (with this placement) is high! Actually, your best channel for expression is in dealing with issues that affect universal rather than personal concerns. This is highly recommended.

Uranus in Virgo. You have original ideas regarding health, science, and technology. You seek your independence through meticulous intellectual research in whatever you undertake. Erratic health problems with this placement may spur you to look into alternative medicine and treatments.

Uranus in Libra. You seek independence through marriage and partnerships. As a result, there may be a tendency for disharmony in your personal relationships. Your unconventional ideas about law and the legal system may prompt you toward reform in that area.

Uranus in Scorpio (exalted). Your independence comes through drastic and profound change in whatever house Uranus in Scorpio occupies. Your temper can be quite fierce, and you may feel compelled to bring about change regardless of the consequences.

Uranus in Sagittarius. Your individuality is expressed through unique concepts in religion, philosophy, education, or spirituality. You seek out the unusual or the eccentric in foreign cultures in an attempt to incorporate other spiritual beliefs into your own.

Uranus in Capricorn. This generation of people (born 1989–1994) will bring about vital changes in government and business power structures. They won't dispense with the past traditions entirely, but will restructure old ideas in new ways. Their ambitions are as strong as their desire to succeed.

Uranus in Aquarius (dignified). You don't hesitate to toss out old ideas and ways of doing things if they no longer work for you. You insist on making your own decisions and value judgments about everything you experience. Your independence is expressed through your impartial intellect and an intuitive sense of how to make connections between seemingly disparate issues.

Back to the Future

Future trends are born in this placement. Actually, Uranus rules Aquarius. Since Uranus deals with personal identity—it's only natural that Aquarius is always redefining himself. He marches to the beat of a different drummer and longs to be noticed for being "unique."

Uranus in Pisces. You bring about change and seek independence through heightened intuition. You have the capacity to delve deeply into the unconscious and receive inspiration through your dreams that you can use in your daily life. Be cautious, however, that your idealism isn't impractical; face and deal with unpleasant situations as they arise.

NEPTUNE AND THE SIGNS

Intuition and Imagination

Neptune spends about twice as long in each sign as Uranus—fourteen years. This makes the sign placement far less important than the house placement, unless Neptune figures prominently in the chart. The sign attests to the capacity of your imagination and your spiritual and intuitive talents. It also addresses the area of your life where you cling to illusions: your blind spots.

Neptune in Aries. This placement fires the imagination on many levels and allows you to act on psychic impulses. Your point of illusion may be your own ego.

Neptune in Taurus. Imagination and spiritual energies are channeled into concrete expression. Your point of illusion can be your own materialism.

Neptune in Gemini. Heightened intuition bridges the left and right brains. Imagination and spiritual issues are channeled through logic and reasoning. Your blind spot may be that you believe you can take on anything. This is a sure route to burnout.

Neptune in Cancer (exalted). The enhanced psychic ability with this placement makes you impressionable. You need to be acutely aware of the fine line between illusion and reality.

Neptune in Leo. Bold creative and artistic concepts characterize this placement. Imagination finds expression in artistic performance. Your ego may hold you hostage.

Neptune in Virgo (detriment). Imagination and spiritual issues are carefully analyzed and fit into a broader, concrete whole for practical use. Strive not to overanalyze.

Neptune in Libra. Imagination and spiritual concepts find expression through beauty and harmony. Misplaced idealism can accompany this placement.

Neptune in Scorpio. Great imagination allows you to pierce the depth of esoteric subjects. You may be blind, however, to your own consuming interest in psychic matters.

Neptune in Sagittarius. Your intuition allows you to understand broad spiritual issues and to fit them into your personal search for truth. Your blind spot may be your need for creative freedom.

Neptune in Capricorn (in fall). Spiritual ideals and concepts are given a practical structure in which to emerge. The risk lies in being so practical that the voice of the imagination is stifled.

Neptune in Aquarius. In a societal sense, heightened intuition and spiritual enlightenment bring about vast and innovative changes and discoveries under this influence.

Neptune in Love

Neptune in Pisces is very difficult in terms of love. This is an idealistic placement—and has trouble seeing a partner for who he truly is. Instead, she sees him as she wants him to be.

Neptune in Pisces (dignified). A vivid imagination allows you to connect to deeper spiritual truths. The risk with this placement is becoming separated from reality and losing yourself in a world of illusion.

PLUTO AND THE SIGNS

Transformation and Regeneration

First, Pluto sweeps in and collapses the old. Then it rebuilds, transforms, and regenerates. The sign it's in describes how your personal transformations are likely to happen; the house placement explains which area of your life is affected. Due to the length of time it spends in a sign, which varies from about twelve to thirty-two years, its personal significance lies primarily in the house it occupies.

Pluto in Aries. It begins the reform, but doesn't have the staying power to finish what it starts. This transit will begin in 2082 and end in 2101. Perhaps the Aries pioneers will be heading out into the solar system to explore new frontiers on other planets.

Pluto in Taurus (detriment). It resists the initial change, yet slides in for the long haul once the process has started. Pluto goes into Taurus in 2101 and stays there for thirty-one years; the Taurean energy will help settle the new frontiers.

Pluto in Gemini. Regeneration manifests through the dissemination of ideas and through communication. In 2132, Pluto will go into Gemini for thirty years. New forms of communication and new ways to disseminate information will be found under this influence.

Pluto in Cancer. Regeneration comes through deep emotional involvement with the home and all that involves the home and homeland. Pluto in this sign will domesticate new worlds.

Pluto in Leo (exalted). Regeneration manifests dramatically through power struggles on an international level. The last time Pluto was in Leo, a power struggle led to World War II. One hopes that when this transit comes around again, war will be obsolete.

Pluto in Virgo. Purging occurs through a careful analysis of what is and isn't essential. Under the last transit in Virgo, great advances were made in medicine and technology. Given the rapid change in both fields, there's no telling where the next transit through Virgo may lead!

Pluto in Libra. Regeneration comes through a revamping of views toward relationships, marriages, and partnerships. By the time this transit comes around again, marriage and family may bear no resemblance at all to what they are now.

Pluto in Scorpio (dignified). This is the eleventh-hour placement of Pluto, which prevailed from 1983 to 1995. AIDS became a terrible reality. Alternative medicine became the most popular kid on the block. Gender, racial, sexual, and legal issues—everything pertinent to our survival as a society and a species—was on the evening news.

Pluto in Sagittarius. In this sign, the transformation will either succeed or fail. If it succeeds, then it's quite possible that we'll be bound as nations through our spiritual beliefs rather than our profit-and-loss statements. If it fails, chaos ensues.

Pluto in Capricorn. With typical Capricorn practicality and discipline, the pieces that Sagittarius spat out will be sculpted and molded into something useful. This will be the reconstruction period of the Aquarian Age.

Pluto in Aquarius (in fall). In 2041, the new order will be ready for Aquarius's humanitarian reforms.

Pluto in Pisces. This begins in 2061, nearly forty-six years in the future. Who besides Nostradamus would presume to predict what might happen? One thing is sure, though: With Pluto in Pisces, we'll at least have a deeper understanding of who and what we are and what makes us all tick.

CHAPTER 6

ADVANCED ASTROLOGY

Now it's time to take what we've learned in preceding chapters and apply it to the practical creation and analysis of astrological materials. Some of the material here may sound pretty technical, but not to worry. It's all part of opening your mind to understand the influences of heavenly bodies.

BIRTH CHARTS

Predicting Your Life

Birth charts are among the most important products of astrology, since they help you to focus various influences and understand how they affect you. A birth chart is circular, with 360 degrees. The ascendant, represented by a horizontal line through the middle of the chart, forms the horizon. The space above it is south of the horizon; the space below it is north. The ascendant (AS) is intersected by the meridian, the axis that connects the Midheaven (MC) and the Nadir or Imum Coeli (IC). The space to the left of the meridian is east; the space to the right is west.

Figure 1

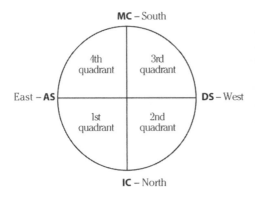

These directions are the opposite of what they usually are because we live in the northern hemisphere, on the "top" of the planet. This means the Sun is due south when it reaches the peak of its daily arc at noon.

The birth chart (Figure 2) shows an ascendant in Pisces, a Sun in Virgo, and a Moon in Virgo. The numbers inside each of the pieces of the pie represent the houses. In the lower left-hand corner is a graph that depicts the various aspects of the chart.

This is a child's chart (1989 birth year). This chart is quite straightforward and shows clearly defined areas of the soul's intent. We'll be referring back to it in later chapters as you begin to put together everything you're learning.

Figure 2

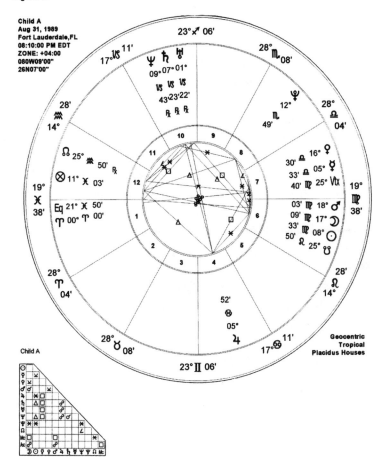

TWELVE HOUSES

The Course of the Year

Think of the sky as a circle. Now divide it into twelve parts. Each "part" is a house. As the Sun travels over the course of a year, it makes a circle, passing from one house to the next. Your Sun sign is where the Sun was on the day you were born, in relation to where you were born, that is, which part of the world. Your ascendant is determined by what hour and minute of the day you were born in relation to this.

House Cusps

The division between one house and another is called the cusp. The sign on the ascendant sets up the structure of the various house cusps. If, for instance, you have Taurus rising—on the cusp of the first house—then Gemini sits on the cusp of your second house, Cancer on the cusp of the third, and so on around the horoscope circle.

The exception to this structure is an "intercepted sign," which means a sign that doesn't appear on the cusp of a house but is completely contained within the house. The chart in Figure 3 shows an interception in the sixth house and in the opposite twelfth house as well. In the first instance, the cusps leap from Virgo on the cusp of the sixth to Scorpio on the cusp of the seventh. Libra has been swallowed. Directly opposite, the cusp of the eleventh house leaps from Taurus on the ascendant to Pisces. Aries has been subsumed.

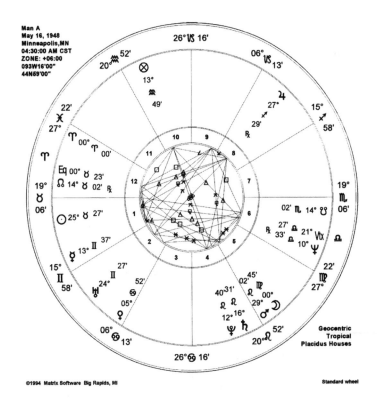

Man A
May 16, 1948
Minneapolis,MN
04:30:00 AM CST
ZONE: +06:00
093W16'00"
44N59'00"

26°♑16'

20°♒52'

⊗ 13°

06°♑13'

49' ♒

27°♐
29°

♃ 27°
15°♐58'

22'
♓
27°

R⃡

♈ 00° ♈ 00'

Eq 00° ♉ 23'
☊ 14° ♉ 02' R⃡

10

11

12

9

8

7

19°
♏
06'

19°
♉
06'

☉ 25° ♉ 27'

1

02° ♏ 14° ☋

R⃡ 27' ♎ 21° Vtx
33' ♎ 10° ♆

☿ 13° ♊ 37'

15°
♊
58'

24° ♊ 52'

⚸ 27'

05° ♊

2

3

4

5

6

♏

♎

22'
♏
27'

40° 31'
♌ ♌
12° 16'

02° 45'
♍
00°
29° ☽

♀

♅ ♄ 52'

♏ 20° ♌

Geocentric
Tropical
Placidus Houses

06°
⊛ 13'

26°♋16'

©1994 Matrix Software Big Rapids, MI

Standard wheel

Interpreting Interceptions

Some astrologers believe an interception portends trouble for the ruler of the intercepted sign. Others think the house that holds the interception is more powerful. Actually, the outcome depends on the overall chart. Sometimes, with an interception, you're attracted to people born under the subsumed sign. Or you manifest those attributes more strongly than you might otherwise.

In the birth chart in Figure 3, ruling planets affected by the interception are Neptune, which rules Pisces, and Mars, which rules Aries.

Each house cusp is ruled by the planet that governs the sign on the cusp. In Figure 3, Taurus is on the ascendant, so Venus rules the first house. Since the Sun is so close to the ascendant in this chart, the Sun could be said to co-rule. Gemini is on the cusp of the second house, so Mercury is the ruler of that house.

However, the natural order of the horoscope begins with Aries, then Taurus, then Gemini, and so on around the zodiac. This means that regardless of what sign is on the cusp, Mars is the natural ruler of the first house because Mars governs Aries. The attributes of the natural rulers must be taken into account when interpreting a chart.

Ascendant Emphasis

The ascendant (AS), or rising sign, is one of the most important features of a natal chart. It's determined by your time of birth. The ascendant determines which planets govern the twelve houses and rules the first house of self. It's the first of the four angles in a chart that you look at in any interpretation.

The horoscope circle is divided into twelve equal parts, numbered counterclockwise. These are the houses that represent certain types of activities and areas of life. The lines that divide the houses are called cusps. The horizontal line that cuts through the middle of the chart is the ascendant. When evaluating a birth chart, notice how planets fall in relation to the horizon or ascendant. A balanced chart has an equal number of planets above and below the horizon.

In Figure 4, six of the ten planets are placed above the horizon. Of the four that lie under the horizon, Mars (♂) and the Moon (☽) are only one and two degrees away from the horizon (the descendant). This is close enough so that their energy is felt in the seventh house as well as the sixth.

With a predominance of planets above the horizon, most experiences for this person are expressed openly. Not much is hidden. This hemisphere is concerned with conscious thought. As astrologer Steven Forrest notes in *The Inner Sky,* "A visible event marks every important developmental milestone on her path. The event may be a move to another city. A marriage. A journey to the East. . . . For such a person there is a perceptible life ritual signaling every major evolutionary step."

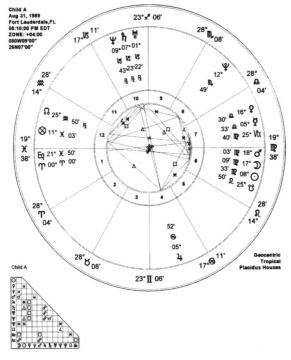

Figure 3

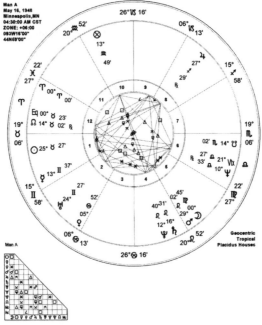

Figure 4

The birth chart in Figure 4 is almost the complete opposite of the one in Figure 3. In Figure 4, all the planets except one are under the horizon. A person with this type of placement is less obvious in what he does and more circumspect.

The imaginary line that divides a chart vertically is called the **MC–IC** or vertical axis. The space to the left of this axis is called the eastern hemisphere; this is where planets are rising. This includes houses one, two, three, ten, eleven, and twelve. The space to the right of the vertical axis is called the western hemisphere; this is the twilight where planets are setting. It includes houses four, five, six, seven, eight, and nine.

People with the majority of their planets to the left of the axis tend to be self-determined; they act on their own choices. Astrologer Robert Hand, however, notes: "The planets in the east should not be ones that, like Saturn, tend to frustrate action, or, like Neptune, weaken the basis on which one should act."

Horizon Placement

Some astrologers say that people who have most of the planets above the horizon tend to be more outgoing, affable, and generally sociable than those who don't. In other words: the first is active, the other is intellectually passive. But this isn't necessarily true! The horizon placement of planets has more to do with how you approach and assimilate experience.

When a majority of the planets lie in the western hemisphere, an individual considers her choices before acting. Opportunities may be somewhat restricted by the society in which the person lives.

The Midheaven and the IC

The Midheaven or **MC** is the highest point in a chart. In Figure 4, this point is 23♐06; in Figure 5, this point is 26♑16. The **IC** lies opposite the Midheaven in the same degree.

Even though the Midheaven doesn't provide much information about the personality, it is vital in understanding someone's life because it pertains to social roles, your public life, your relationship with authority, and status. Since it rules the cusp of the tenth house, which is concerned with an individual's professional life and career, the Midheaven also helps define what a person does for a living.

Any planet that is placed closely to the cusps of the first, fourth, seventh, or tenth houses—the four angles—manifests with considerable strength.

UNDERSTANDING ASPECTS

Angles of Information

To find the aspects in a birth chart, astrologers measure the geometrical distances between the different points. The most important aspect is the conjunction, which is the perfect distance that is created when two planets occupy the same degree (discussed below under Conjunctions). The opposition—created when two planets are 180 degrees apart—is also an essential aspect to know. In this chapter, you'll learn all about aspects, orbs, and other bits and pieces of the astrology puzzle.

As geometric angles between planets, aspects seem rather simple and straightforward. However, they influence everything. Aspects result from the division of the 360 degrees in the horoscope circle.

Symbolically, angles are the network of arteries and veins that link energies between the houses and the planets. They indicate connections between our inner and outer worlds. The square between the North Node and Pluto creates tension—a springboard for growth.

Aspects as Energy

Traditional astrology considers aspects, like planets and houses, in terms of good and bad, difficult or easy. The terminology is actually misleading. Aspects, like planets, are merely representations of certain types of energy. Energy itself is neutral. What we do with the energy is either beneficial or not.

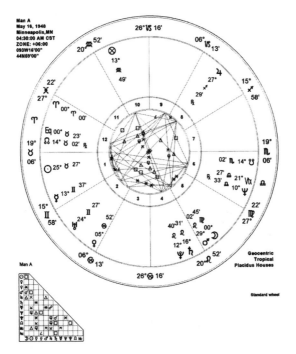

Man A
May 16, 1948
Minneapolis, MN
04:30:00 AM CST
ZONE: +06:00
093W16'00"
44N59'00"

Geocentric
Tropical
Placidus Houses

Man A

Standard wheel

Orbs

The problem with orbs is that astrologers don't generally agree on how many degrees should be allowed for each type of aspect. In *The Inner Sky*, astrologer Steven Forrest writes: "No orb can be defined rigidly. To attempt to nail them down is like trying to determine the exact day on which your kitten became a cat. It doesn't work."

Astrologer Robert Hand considers smaller orbs to generally be more accurate, but is rather philosophical about the whole issue. In *Horoscope Symbols*, he writes: "What the question boils down to is not how far out of orb an aspect can be and still have an effect, but rather how subtle a linkage one will accept as significant." In other words, with practice, you'll arrive at your own sense of how large or small an orb should be.

Rose Lineman and Jan Popelka, writing in *Compendium of Astrology*, use an eight-degree orb for conjunctions and oppositions and smaller orbs for other aspects. Steven Forrest favors orbs of up to five degrees. Although he feels that orbs of six and seven degrees should still be considered, he believes their impact is considerably less. In Forrest's opinion, orbs of eight or nine degrees hardly count. But if an aspect involves the Sun or the Moon, he recommends allowing a wider orb by one or two degrees.

Planets and Orbs

In the past, astrologers assigned particular orbs to particular planets. A Jupiter aspect, for instance, was allowed an orb of ten degrees, which is very wide, considering that the ten degrees applies on either side of the actual degree. In this system, Mercury, Venus, Mars, Saturn, Uranus, Neptune, and Pluto were permitted an eight-degree orb. The Sun got twelve degrees for an orb and the Moon eight.

Most astrology software programs work with orbs between six and eight degrees. If there aren't any tight orbs in the chart, allow orbs of five or six degrees for all aspects. Hand's orbs tend to be smaller than the norm because he uses Midpoints when interpreting a chart.

Aspects Versus Midpoints

A Midpoint is the halfway mark between any two planets. Some astrologers consider Midpoints nearly as important as the aspects themselves.

Take Your Time

Learn about the aspects, but don't worry if it doesn't click right away. It takes time to understand these things. To simplify matters, you can choose to focus on one particular area.

The Aspect Grid

Look at the chart in Figure 6. In the lower left-hand corner, there is a grid with the planet symbols lined up along the edges. The squares of the grid contain the aspect symbols. This is called an "aspect grid" or Aspectarian. Most astrology software programs include them, so you can tell at a glance what aspects a chart contains.

Locate the Sun symbol (☉) along the bottom of the graph. Now locate the **MC** along the left side of the graph. To find out what aspect the Sun and the **MC** make, follow the Sun column up two squares until it's directly opposite the **MC**. You'll see a trine (△).

Defining Aspects

There are numerous minor aspects to consider in a birth chart, but they have far less influence than the major ones. The minor aspects can also be a bit confusing when you're just starting out. So, it's recommended that you don't use them until you've mastered the major aspects. Concentrate on those discussed in the following few pages for now.

MOON AND SUN CONJUNCTIONS

Joined Energies

Conjunction is the simplest aspect to identify, but it's also one of the most complex because of the intensity and power involved. Whenever you see two or more planets piled on top of each other, usually, but not always, in the same house, their energies fuse and intensify. If the orb is exact or within one degree, the impact is considerable.

When interpreting conjunctions, understand that they fuse and intensify planetary energies. Relate the conjunctions to the houses in which they are found. Then dig deeper to find out more about yourself!

Conjunctions of the Sun

Conjunctions of the Sun act as a magnifying glass to intensify and focus solar energy. The essence of a conjuncting planet doesn't just blend with that of the Sun; it unites with it, enhancing and strengthening its (solar) energy.

Burnout or Manifestation?

There are at least two schools of thought on conjunctions of the Sun. The first holds that the planet's energy is burned up by the Sun. The second theory is that the solar energy becomes a perfect vehicle for the manifestation of that planet's energy. Both theories can apply—it depends on the overall chart.

If a planet lies within half a degree to four degrees from the Sun, it's said to be combust. This means exactly what it sounds like: The planet's energy breaks down and is essentially absorbed by the solar energy. If a planet is less than half a degree from the Sun, it's said to be cazimi (in the heart of).

Sun Conjunct Moon. You get what you want through a perfect blend of will and ego. You have strong ties with your family, spouse, and home.

Sun Conjunct Mercury. Your will is focused through your intellect. You act on your ideas and make them happen.

Sun Conjunct Venus. You're definitely a lover: A lover of life, beauty, music, and art; a lover of love. On the downside, you may have a tendency toward laziness and self-indulgence.

Sun Conjunct Mars. You're aggressive, self-motivated, and bold. You're also outspoken and blunt, which sometimes proves to be an advantage, but usually gets you into trouble.

Competitive!

Having the Sun conjunct Mars can give you a real competitive streak. Sexually, it can make you adventurous and daring—you'll try anything once!

Sun Conjunct Jupiter. Even in adverse times, you're naturally lucky. Your self-confidence and self-reliance always bring you more than you need.

Sun Conjunct Saturn. This aspect either provides the structure and discipline you need to achieve prominence, or it oppresses you so deeply that you always feel a tinge of melancholy. Responsibility is thrust on you at an early age that might cause you to withdraw into yourself.

Sun Conjunct Uranus. Through flashes of insight and an instinctive understanding of divine laws, you have the ability to venture into unexplored realms and impact the world with what you find.

Celebrate Difference!

Uranus deals with the unexpected and marching to the beat of a different drummer. If your Sun is conjunct Uranus, it means that you're an original, creative thinker, though you tend to want everything done perfectly.

Sun Conjunct Neptune. Your strong mystical bent, used constructively, can trigger enormous creativity. The downside to this aspect is scattered mental and emotional energy, a fascination with or overindulgence in drugs or alcohol, and a tendency to daydream.

Sun Conjunct Pluto. Your powerful will regenerates and transforms everything it touches. Sexual and mental energy are usually your vehicles for transformation.

Sun Conjunct North Node. Your opportunities for self-expression are greatly enhanced and can manifest itself as leadership and power. The luck inherent to this aspect is something you've earned through past lives.

Sun Conjunct South Node. Circumstances in your life either deny or limit your chances for self-expression. The house placement tells which area is affected.

Sun Conjunct Ascendant. Imagine vitality at its peak—illness is as rare as water in the Mojave Desert. Even when you do get sick, you recuperate quickly and completely.

Luck Comes Your Way

If you know your Part of Fortune and your Sun conjuncts this, then you're in luck—literally. In other words, your luck and success come through personal efforts, in the area represented by the house that the Part of Fortune occupies.

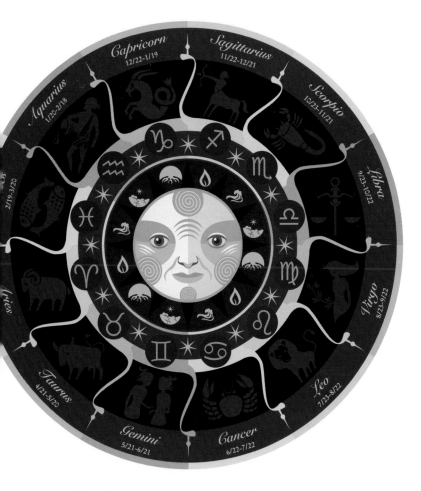

The great wheel of the zodiac, showing the signs encircling the Sun.

Astrology was developed in ancient Babylon in Mesopotamia. Perhaps astrologers studied the stars from one of the city-state's great towers.

Among the earliest writers on astrology was the Greek mathematician Claudius Ptolemy. He also formulated a cosmological system that held sway in astronomy until the fifteenth century.

Ptolemäos 1. Lagos

Fig. 68.—Astronomer accused of Sorcery, holding a Disc with Magic Figures.—Capital Letter in a " Book of Jurisprudence."—Manuscript of the Thirteenth Century.

During the Middle Ages, the church often attacked astrology. Here, in a manuscript from the thirteenth century, an astrologer accused of sorcery holds a disc with magical figures on it.

Although the church opposed astrology, astrological symbols often made their way into ecclesiastical architecture. Here we see the sign of Scorpio on the outside of the Cathédrale Notre Dame d'Amiens in France.

Photo credit: © iStockphoto.com/digitalimagination

'IN THE RIGHT SEASON.'

In the Renaissance, astrology flourished through the contributions of philosophers such as Marsilio Ficino. At the same time, it began to part ways with astronomy, its more scientific cousin.

Photo credit: © iStockphoto.com/ZU_09

Devices such as this armillary sphere were used by Renaissance astrologers to plot the movement of the signs through the heavens.

A clock tower in Venice. The winged lion, symbol of St. Mark, stares benevolently down at the zodiacal clock.

Photo credit: © iStockphoto.com/Baloncici

Looking more closely at the Venetian clock, we can see the symbols of the zodiac as they make their way around a star-filled sky that includes the Sun and Moon.

Photo credit: © iStockphoto.com/TeodoraDjordjevic

The astronomical clock in Prague, showing astrological symbols on the inner dial. This is the third-oldest clock of its kind and the only one still in working order.

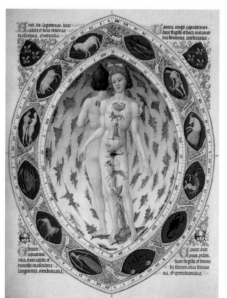

Throughout the Middle Ages, as can be seen from this manuscript illumination, astrologers eagerly studied the skies for portents and wrote elaborate commentaries on Classical texts about astrology.

A sundial, a common ornament in many gardens, shows the ongoing influence of astrology, as the zodiac appears on the inner part of the dial.

The symbols of the twelve houses of the zodiac have fascinated students of astrology for more than 2,000 years.

Sun Conjunct Midheaven. You seek fame, acclaim, and the realization of your professional abilities. However your fame manifests, it's sure to impact the masses.

Sun Conjunct IC. Family and home are paramount in your life. You have a deep appreciation of your early life, family roots, and values.

Conjunctions of the Moon

Conjunctions of the Moon heighten the emotions and unconscious mind. It represents your subconscious. This aspect always involves women and relationships with women. It also governs instinctive reactions to events and situations indicated by sign and house placement.

Moon Conjunct Mercury. If well-aspected, you have an excellent memory and heightened intuition. If poorly aspected, you are restless and are excessively sensitive to criticism.

Moon Conjunct Venus. If you're a woman, you're successful in romance and friendships and with women in general. If this is a man's chart, this aspect is all about the kind of sparkling personality that makes other people feel good when they're around you.

Moon Conjunct Mars. Your emotions are intense, and you have a quick, expressive intellect. Combined with a Venus conjunction, you may develop into a great artist or musician. Generally, this aspect suggests fortunate financial affairs.

Moon Conjunct Jupiter. Your sympathetic and generous nature wins you friends among many different kinds of people. You enjoy travel, particularly if it's with family members or people who are like kin to you.

Moon Conjunct Saturn. Your nature is rather serious and thoughtful. You tend to be introverted, may be emotionally repressed, and sometimes act as if you're the center of the universe.

Moon Conjunct Uranus. You're a complete original: eccentric, independent, and fearless. You often behave so unpredictably that people don't know what to expect from you.

Moon Conjunct Neptune. You're psychically attuned to other people, to their emotional environments. Depending on other aspects in the chart, there can be mental and emotional confusion or heightened mediumistic tendencies that can provide spiritual insight.

Moon Conjunct Pluto. Your emotions are so intense that other people may have trouble handling you for long periods of time. Your willingness to take emotional risks results in a periodic purging of your most intimate relationships.

Moon Conjunct North Node. You've got your finger on the public pulse and use this to your advantage. Your relationships with women are generally good and beneficial to you in some way.

Moon Conjunct South Node. Your timing isn't good. You somehow miss being in the right place at the right time. This may lead to depression, bitterness, and, ultimately, isolation.

Moon Conjunct Ascendant. You empathize with others. Your early childhood experiences are carried with you throughout your life and color your emotional responses as an adult.

Moon Conjunct Midheaven. If you're not living your life in the public eye now, you will at some point in your life. Women are helpful in achieving your goals.

Moon Conjunct IC. Your strong family ties support you emotionally. Your intuition is well developed, particularly when it pertains to your children, parents, family, and home.

CONJUNCTIONS OF THE PLANETS

Finding Your Group

Just as the Sun and Moon can conjunct with planets and nodes, so the planets can group together and affect one another's influence. As with the Sun and Moon, the extent of that influence will be affected by the degree of conjunction.

Mercury

Mercury conjunctions energize the intellect and clarify and validate mental processes. Also, Mercury conjunctions show our true communication skills.

Mercury Conjunct Venus. You have literary talent and a deep appreciation of the arts in general. You're a soft-spoken individual, with a facility for communicating your ideas.

Mercury Conjunct Mars. You speak your mind, act on your decisions, and enjoy debating about controversial issues. You may have a tendency to allow debate to collapse into heated arguments in which you passionately defend your position, even if it's wrong.

Mercury Conjunct Jupiter. It's as if you were born knowing right from wrong; there are no gray areas for you. You have a deep interest in religion, spiritual issues, the law, and education.

Mercury Conjunct Saturn. Your innate understanding of structure and form gives you a powerful capacity for visualization. It may delay recognition in your profession, but your careful planning and foresight win in the end.

Mercury Conjunct Uranus. Your intuitive flashes allow you to perceive things that other people miss. This inspiration provides you with original solutions to issues and problems.

Mercury Conjunct Neptune. Your imagination is a central and complex part of your life. You may write poetry, music, or mystical fiction, a creatively beneficial outlet for this aspect.

Channel Your Psychic Input

Neptune is the planet of idealism, and it makes us lose sight of what is real and what is imagined. In other words, if you have your Mercury conjunct Neptune, make sure to carefully channel this psychic input. If you don't, it could hurl you into a surreal world where you could eventually lose touch with reality.

Mercury Conjunct Pluto. Your enormous willpower and resourcefulness allow you to penetrate to the truth of whatever it is you need and want to understand. You would make a terrific detective or scientist who works with classified or secret information.

Mercury Conjunct North Node. You're in the flow; aware of what the public seeks. You can become an intellectual leader or spokesperson for a particular idea or set of ideals. You evolve through your communication skills.

Mercury Conjunct South Node. Your timing is off. You're either behind the times or ahead of them. This can lead to deep frustration, but that's the easy way out. Persevere and your originality will win out.

Mercury Conjunct Ascendant. You're very bright, high strung, and maddeningly logical. Once you apply your intellect to what you want, you succeed far beyond your own expectations.

Plan, Plan, Plan!

If your Mercury conjuncts your Part of Fortune (remember, it's where your luck lies), here's some good advice: Plan well, use your resources, and look to the house the Part of Fortune occupies to understand where to direct your energies.

Mercury Conjunct Midheaven. Career, business, and professional ambition are your areas of interest. Publishing, journalism, writing, any kind of communication profession would suit you.

Mercury Conjunct IC. You come from a well-educated family where intellectual achievements are recognized and honored. You love books and your home is probably filled with them.

Venus

Any planet that conjuncts Venus influences your social behaviors, including your friendships and your acquaintances. This will also tell more about what kind of artistic expression fascinates and defines you.

Venus Conjunct Mars. Your passionate nature gets you involved in many different types of relationships, not all of them good for you. You're lucky in financial matters, and you have a good time spending money.

Venus Conjunct Jupiter. You're cheerful, optimistic, sociable, and kind toward other people. You probably support religious or spiritual causes and help people who are less fortunate than you.

Don't Get Complacent

On the downside, when Venus conjuncts Jupiter, things can be too easy, which can lead to indolence, self-indulgence, and laziness! If Saturn is prominent in your chart, it will add structure and discipline to the overall horoscope and create a channel for using this aspect positively.

Venus Conjunct Saturn. Romantic relationships are serious business for you. Your adherence to tradition may compel you to stay in a relationship long after it no longer works. Divorce is rare with this aspect.

Venus Conjunct Uranus. Your romantic relationships are unconventional and probably begin and end suddenly. The line between friendship and love can be quite blurred for you at times. Your earning and spending habits are marked by the same erratic tendencies as your love life.

Venus Conjunct Neptune. Your physical beauty reflects the mystical and spiritual traits inherent to this conjunction. People are drawn to your gentleness, sensitivity, and elusive spiritual nature. You love music and art that are mystically inspired.

Venus Conjunct Pluto. Sexual magnetism and tremendous passion mark this aspect. In self-aware individuals, this aspect can lead to the height of spiritual love and compassion, which transforms everyone who comes in contact with it.

Venus Conjunct North Node. You have a knack for being in the right place at the right time. Through social contacts you develop because of this, you attract what you need for personal fulfillment and success.

Venus Conjunct South Node. You feel emotionally isolated much of the time, but it's due to your own behavior patterns. Try to develop a more acute sense of timing in your social interactions.

Venus Conjunct Ascendant. Physically you're a knockout, especially if you're a woman. You can charm your way into getting virtually anything you want.

Smooth Love Life

If your Venus happens to conjunct your Part of Fortune, your love life should be smooth sailing! You benefit financially through marriage and partnerships in general. You gain through love.

Venus Conjunct Midheaven. Social ambition is what this aspect is about. It's a wonderful aspect for artists, publicists, and diplomats. You attract money and power through social contacts and relationships.

Venus Conjunct IC. Your life is about creating, maintaining, and enjoying domestic harmony. Your marriage and family are important to you, as are your parents and early childhood.

Mars

With Mars conjunctions, think activity: It has to do with your energy levels and the way you deal with work and the people around you. Mars conjunctions will also give away your aggressiveness. This conjunction will also show what your sexual appetite and tendencies are like.

Mars Conjunct Jupiter. You have few equals in terms of energy and enthusiasm, particularly when you're dealing with something you feel passionate about. Whenever you're told that something can't be done or that you can't do something, you proceed to prove everyone wrong.

Mars Conjunct Saturn. Your physical endurance surpasses that of many of your contemporaries. You work hard and long to achieve what you desire.

Mars Conjunct Uranus. You despise boredom and are constantly looking for thrills and chills. Your daredevil attitude can lead into extremism and rebellion against authority and any restriction of your personal freedom.

Mars Conjunct Neptune. In self-aware people, this conjunction unites physical and spiritual energy. In practical terms, this means that psychic healing ability may be evident and that you have the innate capacity to manifest what you desire.

Beware Drugs and Alcohol!

If your Mars conjuncts your Neptune, impractical goals, scattered energy, and peculiar romantic involvements may result. If your Mars conjuncts Neptune, be advised to stay clear of drugs and alcohol and to maintain good health through diet and exercise.

Mars Conjunct Pluto. This aspect gives incredible physical strength and a powerful personal magnetism. If Mars is more prominent, then the power is expressed through baser emotions: lust, greed, and achievement at the expense of others.

With Pluto dominant, you have the capacity to transform and regenerate yourself in such a way that your voice becomes that of a spiritual leader.

Mars Conjunct North Node. You're in step with the times and in harmony with your personal environment. Your drive to succeed (look to the house placement to find out which area is affected) allows you to overcome any restrictions imposed by the sign and house placement of the South Node.

Mars Conjunct South Node. You may object to the military values of the country in which you live and to many of the current trends. Your sense of timing may be off, and, because of this, you may unknowingly antagonize others.

Mars Conjunct Ascendant. You've got all the Mars traits: aggression, energy, initiative, and impulsiveness. On the downside, you may also be reckless and accident-prone.

Mars Conjunct Midheaven. You're focused on your career and professional achievements and pour a lot of energy into attaining prominence. You're extremely competitive and don't shrink away from the task at hand when confronted with setbacks.

Mars Conjunct IC. Disharmony in the home and family life is indicated unless Mars is well-aspected or you work out of your home.

Jupiter

It's important to look at the aspects made to these conjunctions. If they're good, then the terrific, expansive qualities of Jupiter dominate. If the conjunction is badly aspected, then look for extravagance and excess.

Jupiter Conjunct Saturn. This aspect, which comes around about once every twenty years, means you probably have to overcome major obstacles to expand the affairs of the house where the conjunction falls.

Jupiter Conjunct Uranus. This one rolls around every fourteen years or so. It means that you experience sudden and unexpected opportunities to expand in whatever area the house placement rules. You may travel suddenly.

Jupiter Conjunct Neptune. Look for this aspect every thirteen years. You're imaginative, have a distinct spiritual or mystical bent, and possess some sort of psychic talent that you should develop.

Jupiter Conjunct Pluto. This powerful aspect can work constructively or destructively. You either seek to achieve goals that benefit not only yourself but others as well, or you're a power monger.

Develop Your Spiritual Side

With those who are more emotionally mature or self-aware, Jupiter conjunct Pluto is a good reason for learning about and fully developing your spiritual side. Beneficial practices include: yoga, meditation, metaphysical studies, and spiritual healing.

Jupiter Conjunct North Node. This is a terrific aspect, particularly if you're involved with the public. Your beliefs are in tune with current trends.

Jupiter Conjunct South Node. You feel blocked much of the time—restricted or limited—just as you would with a Jupiter-Saturn conjunction. Look to the house placement of the North Node to understand how to overcome the challenges of this aspect.

Jupiter Conjunct Ascendant. Your optimism inspires others, who may look to you as an authority of some kind. Your main passions revolve around education, legal, or spiritual concerns.

Jupiter Conjunct Midheaven. This is a fine aspect for achieving professional recognition and success. It's often found in the horoscopes of politicians, attorneys, educators, anyone in the public eye.

Jupiter Conjunct IC. You're a builder—either literally or figuratively. This aspect is good for real estate brokers and anyone in the home construction, improvement, or decoration business.

Saturn

Saturn conjunctions can restrict and limit the flow of energy between planets or can discipline and structure the energies to create a single-minded purpose or goal.

Saturn Conjunct Uranus. This aspect happens every ninety-one years. In evolved individuals, it suggests the ability to funnel original and unconventional ideas into practical use and application.

Muddled Thinking

On the darker side, the conjunction of Saturn and Uranus can lead to muddled thinking, a temper that flares periodically (and is nearly impossible to control), and a lack of distinction between the real and the imagined.

Saturn Conjunct Neptune. You're clairvoyant and possess tremendous spiritual insight. Your compassion extends to all living things. This is a lucky aspect, which usually indicates financial fortune.

Saturn Conjunct Pluto. With this powerful aspect, the intense Plutonian energy is structured through Saturn. This gives concrete expression to your ambitions, for which you're willing to work long, hard, and patiently.

Saturn Conjunct North Node. You thrive in a conservative environment and follow protocol to the letter. With the South Node opposing, you must work to overcome your prejudices.

Saturn Conjunct South Node. You're too rigid for your own good. It holds you back professionally and personally. Loosen up or decide what it is you want and go after it!

Saturn Conjunct Ascendant. Life for you is serious business. You're responsible, a hard worker, and conscientious in all you do.

Saturn Conjunct Midheaven. You're headed for the big time, but only through hard work and perseverance. Recognition is likely to come after the age of forty.

Saturn Conjunct IC. Saturn here usually indicates an emotionally detached relationship with your parents. You feel conflicted and torn between your professional ambitions and your duty to your parents and/or family.

Uranus

Like conjunctions of Saturn, Neptune, and Pluto, conjunctions of Uranus have broad effects on generations of people because they're such slow-moving planets.

Uranus, Neptune, and Pluto are farther away than most other planets. As such, they represent how the soul's individual choices merge and meld with the shaping of nations, cultures, and the family of man.

Uranus Conjunct Neptune. This one occurs every 171 years or so. It occurred most recently in 1994, so children born under this conjunction will make incredible strides in psychic and spiritual development.

Uranus Conjunct Pluto. Blame this aspect for revolution. It's responsible for the overthrow of governments and the collapse of outdated belief paradigms. It comes along about every 115 years.

Uranus Conjunct North Node. You're quick to spot new trends in science and technology, the arts, films, and any endeavor that deals with the masses.

Uranus Conjunct South Node. Your life is disrupted by changing mores, beliefs, and trends. Unless you roll with the punches, you're in for a tough ride.

Uranus Conjunct Ascendant. You're exceptionally bright. Your IQ may even shoot into the genius range. You're also incredibly eccentric, with unusual tastes.

Uranus Conjunct Midheaven. You do best as your own boss. If well-aspected, overnight success may result. But this can be followed just as quickly by obscurity. Play your cards wisely, carefully, and nurture your intuitive voice.

Uranus Conjunct IC. Your parents and/or home are peculiar in some way, and there are a lot of odd people coming and going. Electronic gadgets and cutting edge computer technology may be present.

Unexpected Luck

If you're lucky enough to know that your Uranus conjuncts the Part of Fortune, then you know that your luck often comes in spurts, at unexpected moments, and probably when you need it most. If you learn to recognize synchronicities and attempt to understand what they're telling you, you'll stay ahead of the surprise game.

Neptune

Neptune conjunctions, like those of Saturn, Uranus, and Pluto, affect generations of people. They enhance psychic and spiritual development, imagination, and intuition. They bolster artistic ability and compassion.

Neptune Conjunct Pluto. Somewhere in the twenty-fourth century, this conjunction will roll around again. It usually means spiritual revolution and rebirth with Pluto's capacity for constructive or destructive tendencies. It also usually coincides with the rise and fall of cultures and nations.

Neptune Conjunct North Node. Relax and follow your intuitive urges. If you do, you'll always be in the right place at the right time and make the right contacts.

Neptune Conjunct South Node. You say the wrong things at the wrong times. You have trouble getting your act together. Put one foot in front of the other, maintain your individualism, and never forget that you create your own reality.

Neptune Conjunct Ascendant. You've got a lot of psychic talent, but unless you develop and work with it, the talent lies latent. Guard against drug and alcohol abuse.

Neptune Conjunct Midheaven. Your career ambitions may be impractical and unrealistic. And that's the point with this conjunction. Listen to your intuitive voice. Heed its guidance.

Neptune Conjunct IC. Your spiritual passions enter your home. You're mystically inclined, with the heart of a pagan who feels a kindred link with the planet and cosmos.

Pluto

All aspects of Pluto bear a disturbing similarity to marriage vows: "for better or worse, until death do us part." The conjunction is no different.

Pluto's Direct Effects

Pluto's impact on us depends to a large degree on how consciously aware we are. In other words, the planetary energy tends to hit us in the area of our lives where we most need to change so that we can grow and evolve as spiritual beings. Pay attention to it, and you'll come out ahead!

One of the popular notions among astrologers is that Pluto aspects don't affect you personally unless Pluto is strong in your chart. When Pluto moved into Sagittarius at the end of 1995, many people went through monumental changes in their lives. Other people sailed through the transition with hardly a ripple in their lives.

Pluto Conjunct North Node. Take nothing for granted. Scrutinize the hidden elements in your life. Seek to understand what isn't obvious, and you'll be way ahead of the game.

Pluto Conjunct South Node. You work alone to transform your life. You may be a part of mass events that wipe your security slate utterly clean, forcing you to start over again and again. And when you finally figure out the pattern, you break it and evolve.

Pluto Conjunct Ascendant. Each of us possesses the capacity for good and evil. The manifestation of one or the other depends entirely on our free will. That's what this aspect is about: free will.

Pluto Conjunct Midheaven. You reinvent yourself professionally and publicly, time and again, until you get the message. This powerful aspect leads to fame or notoriety, either/or. That's how Pluto works.

Pluto Conjunct IC. It's not easy, and it's not fun. But one way or another you learn to deal with change and transformation in your home life, or you will repeat this pattern over and over. And that's nothing to write home about.

SPECIAL ASPECT PATTERNS

Five Patterns to Look For

Several aspects can combine to create particular patterns that change or enhance the original aspect. There are five such patterns you should look for when interpreting any birth chart: stellium, T-square, grand square or grand cross, grand trine or cosmic cross, and kite.

Stellium

This is a cluster of stars within the same sign or house or within a certain orb in adjacent houses. The key here is to pay special attention to any sign or house that contains three or more planets. In Figure 5, note the stellium of five planets in the first house. Four of the planets—Sun (☉), Jupiter (♃), Venus (♀), and Mercury (☿)—are in Aquarius. Even though the Moon (☽) is in Pisces, it's conjunct the Sun at a five-degree orb, so it should be considered in the overall impact of the stellium.

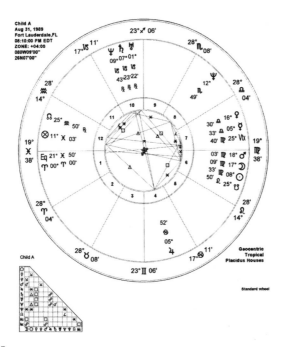

Figure 5

In the eighth house, there are three planets: Mars (♂), Neptune (♆), and Saturn (♄). The planets are in Libra and Virgo and aren't conjunct, unless you take into account a wide seven-degree orb between Mars and Neptune. But toss in the South Node (☋), and we find that eight out of the ten planets and two out of the three points fall within two houses. Now these three planets in the eighth house—even though they aren't conjunct by sign or degree—assume a vital importance.

At a glance, the stellium in the first house immediately tells us the individual's perception of the world is heavily colored by subjectivity. She probably has a clear sense of herself—who she is and where she's going. Her interaction with the world is expressed through the affairs of the eighth house. Not surprisingly, this woman was an attorney for many years and is now a family court judge.

T-Square

This pattern is formed when two or more planets are in opposition and square a third planet. The third planet becomes the center of tension and represents the challenge the individual faces. It's often found in the charts of prominent individuals.

Grand Square or Grand Cross

This pattern is an extension of the T-square. Created by four squares and two oppositions, the pattern has at least one planet in each of the quadruplicities: fixed, cardinal, or mutable. This pattern is one of extreme tension and represents difficult challenges. But when the energies are used correctly, the pattern can lead to enormous strength.

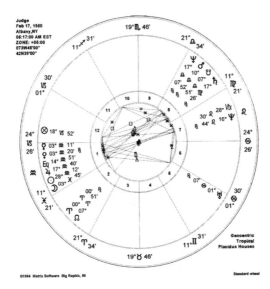

Figure 6

Grand Trine or Cosmic Cross

Look for three planets that occupy different signs of the same element at 120-degree angles. This auspicious aspect in a chart indicates tremendous creativity expressed through the element of the trine. Too many trines in a chart actually indicate that the individual may lack focus and ambition.

Trine Enhancements

A Water trine enhances psychic ability, receptivity, and compassion. A Fire trine increases initiative and drive. An Earth trine brings material abundance. An Air trine intensifies intellectual ability and expression.

Kite

This pattern is an extension of the Grand Trine. A fourth planet forms an opposition to one corner of the triangle, thus sextiling the other two corners.

Applying Versus Separating Aspects

Due to the different rates at which planets move, some aspects in a chart are applying or forming, and others are separating or moving away from an exact aspect. Applying aspects have more impact than those that are separating.

Forming and Separating Aspects

When an aspect is forming, it means that conditions, events, circumstances, emotions, or states of mind become evident as a person moves through life. Separating aspects pinpoint elements of an individual's experiences that are part of his nature at birth and may include karmic conditions and relationships.

In terms of their speed, from faster to slower, the planets line up with the Moon leading the procession, followed by Mercury, Venus, Sun, Mars, Jupiter, Saturn, Uranus, Neptune, and Pluto.

SUN AND MOON SQUARES
Tension Creates Action

Squares tell a great deal about the challenges a soul chooses before it is born into physical reality. They spur us to action because the points of friction they create are difficult to ignore. Squares create a kind of terrible itch in certain areas of our lives that compels us to do something in order to change the status quo.

Sun Squares

Look at your own chart. What planets and houses are involved in the squares? What do these particular planets and houses tell you about yourself? How can you work with the friction to alleviate it? Sometimes a square will spur us on and make us stronger—less lazy and more willing to demand what we can from ourselves. The following are Sun squares. Note that there can never be a Sun square Mercury or Venus.

Sun Square Moon. Your conscious mind constantly battles with your emotions over what you want and how you should achieve your goals. To meet the challenge, you must bring old behavioral patterns that may have originated during your childhood to light.

Sun Square Mars. You're hot-tempered. It takes a lot to make you mad, but when you reach that flashpoint, you explode. You're also argumentative, passionate, and energetic.

Sun Square Jupiter. You make a comfortable living, but spend money as fast as it comes in. Your excesses may cause you problems of all sorts, particularly through ill health in later years. Your humanity, however, remains constant.

Sun Square Saturn. You struggle to succeed and yet, at every turn, your efforts seem to be thwarted. But your ambition, pierced by inner friction, drives you forward.

Sun Square Uranus. Your powerful, creative urges often frustrate you because they come in spurts. You must develop perseverance and discipline so you can structure this force and work with it regularly.

Sun Square Neptune. Self-delusion may be your undoing. Guard against mystical feelings of grandeur, avoid cults of any type, and seek to cultivate your reasoning, left-brain faculties.

Sun Square Pluto. This one is difficult. Pluto creates so much inner friction, your need to achieve overwhelms nearly everything else in your life. But if the friction is turned inward, toward transforming the self, the darker elements in this square are greatly mitigated.

Sun Square Nodes. This aspect forms a T-square. It can be a dynamic aspect, one that propels you forward. To overcome this, you need to nurture the part of your life described by the house your Sun occupies.

Sun Square Ascendant. You're conflicted about projecting yourself as you really are. It creates problems in your closest relationships because no one seems to understand you. To overcome this, cultivate the area of your life described by the house the Sun occupies.

Sun Square Midheaven. You don't get along with the authority figures in your life. Your professional ambitions may be stymied somehow by your family obligations.

Moon Squares

Moon squares often indicate unconscious blocks, prejudices, and habits that impede your emotional expression. This can affect your health, particularly in a woman's chart.

Moon Square Mercury. You talk too much. But you're so witty and glib that people usually enjoy your company anyway. The problem, though, is that you may talk about things that should be better kept to yourself. Overcome this challenge by being more circumspect in your speech.

Moon Square Venus. You feel inferior to others, and this prompts you to indulge in all sorts of detrimental habits. You spend your money foolishly, allow yourself to be taken advantage of, and aren't very sociable. Think before you act, and strive to overcome your feelings of inferiority.

Moon Square Mars. You take things much too personally, which fuels your emotionally volatile nature. Your independence often runs to the extreme, creating problems with your parents when you were younger and with your own family, later.

Moon Squares in Childhood

According to accomplished astrologer Grant Lewi, a Moon square Mars will often manifest itself as early as childhood. Other aspects won't necessarily be pronounced so early on. This aspect shows itself as precociousness in early childhood.

Moon Square Jupiter. You're a sucker for a sob story. You go overboard with everyone you love and even with people you don't know. But you can afford your extravagances because you believe you'll always have more than you need.

Moon Square Saturn. Astrologers generally view this aspect unfavorably, saying that it leads to depression, melancholy, and emotional coldness. But Grant Lewi has a different take on it: "This is perhaps the most powerful single aspect you can have in a horoscope. It gives both ambition and the ability to concentrate on it."

Moon Square Uranus. You're emotionally restless, flitting from one thing to another in search of the ultimate. Your talents are exceptional and reflect your individualism. Once you understand what they're trying to tell you about yourself and your life, you break the pattern.

Moon Square Neptune. You're a daydreamer who spins wonderful tales and fantasies. But you're so impractical, you don't know how to make these flights of fancy into concrete achievements. Don't surrender your imagination, instead channel it in constructive ways.

Moon Square Pluto. Don't be so intense! Life isn't always an either/or proposition. Use your psychic abilities and intense emotions to bring about a more gradual change in your life.

Moon Square Nodes. This T-square configuration urges you to overcome emotional or unconscious habits and prejudices. Until you do, you run into problems with women and can't fulfill your ambitions.

Moon Square Ascendant. You have trouble expressing yourself emotionally. As a result, you experience difficulties in partnerships, marriages, and with your family. If you can become aware of your habitual attitudes and patterns of behavior, you're on your way to breaking them and freeing yourself.

Moon Square Midheaven and IC. Domestic problems seem to get in the way of your professional ambitions. This leads to frustration, which only compounds the original problems. The source of the trouble lies somewhere in your unconscious behavioral patterns.

Moon Square Part of Fortune. Your emotional frustration detracts from the areas of life in which you're lucky. Dig deep within to find the habitual patterns that are holding you back.

PLANETARY SQUARES
Creating Friction for Creativity

No single aspect makes or breaks a chart. With a square or any other aspect, you need to look at how it fits with the rest of the horoscope. In one person, an aspect may very well lead to depression and ill health. But in someone else, it can be the trigger that spurs the individual to great professional heights.

Mercury Squares

These squares create friction, intellectually, through all types of communication. They also create friction with siblings and neighbors. Look to the houses and signs to understand where the intellectual abilities aren't being developed to their fullest. Mercury and Venus can only form a conjunction and a sextile because they are never 47 degrees away from each other.

Mercury Square Mars. Your sharp tongue often borders on outright rudeness. It tends to alienate the very people whose support you need. Take time to gather the facts and plan what you're going to say before you say it.

Mercury Square Jupiter. Your mind is rich and imaginative, but your judgment is often flawed because you either misinterpret or don't have all the facts. The best way to overcome the challenges of this aspect is through education, books, and any kind of mental training.

Mercury Square Saturn. You're a thinker with a profound mind able to grasp complex issues. But you think and worry too much, dwelling on past injustices and injuries. This may create negative and prejudicial attitudes that ultimately hold you back.

Break Your Patterns

In order to overcome the challenge of this Mercury Square Saturn, you need to break with your habitual patterns. Forgive people who have injured you. Strive to consider other people's feelings before you act. This will make your life so much better.

Mercury Square Uranus. Mentally, you're way ahead of the pack. Your insight can be brilliant and original. Your entire thought process is radical and independent but sometimes so unfocused that your energy ends up scattered and wasted. Slow down, think before you act and speak.

Mercury Square Neptune. This aspect favors fiction writing, particularly of the mystical variety. It also gives insight into the motives and behaviors of other people, which is helpful in creating interesting fictional characters. Writing or art are constructive ways to channel the challenges of this square.

Mercury Square Pluto. You're able to assess a given situation swiftly and accurately. Your willpower is well developed, and you may try to force your ideas on others. You don't take anything anyone says at face value; you need to prove the truth to yourself.

Mercury Square Nodes. Think before you speak. Otherwise, you may speak at the wrong time and will be sorely misunderstood. Take a deeper interest in the world you inhabit.

Mercury Square Ascendant. It's difficult for you to express yourself verbally or in writing. You benefit from training in speech and writing, through education, workshops, and anything that provides a structure. This, in turn, improves your relationships with the important people in your life.

Mercury Square Midheaven. Your communication skills are flawed, and this creates disharmony at home and on the job. The misunderstandings that result make you miserable. Seek educational training in these areas.

Venus Squares

These squares generally create friction in relationships. They also affect finances: the way you spend and the way you regard money, in general. Venus squares can also indicate enhanced artistic ability. They also show you the lessons you need to learn and grow from in love.

Venus Square Mars. You often find yourself in stormy romantic relationships that go nowhere. You use other people for sexual gratification or you are used yourself. To overcome the challenge of this square, you must cultivate temperance and balance.

Venus Square Jupiter. You're seduced by the pleasures in life and tend to be extravagant in everything you do. To overcome the challenge of this square, you need to pull back from your life and scrutinize it with detachment.

Venus Square Saturn. Your fear of poverty colors everything you do and feel. You're probably at your best when you're alone. To overcome this challenge, bring your fears to the surface and deal with them.

Venus Square Uranus. Your love life is marked by sudden changes, abrupt beginnings and endings, and unusual, sudden attractions. You need to honestly assess what you're looking for in life and pursue it diligently, and with forethought.

Venus Square Neptune. Your artistic abilities are excellent and can provide you with a creative outlet for much of the friction caused by this square. Your imagination is fueled by the forbidden, and, as a result, you may get involved in secret love affairs. You need to come to terms with what you need emotionally, and then try to create it in your life.

Venus Square Pluto. Your sexual passions nearly swallow up the rest of your life. You attract people who may be involved in illegal activities. This square doesn't favor harmonious marriages or partnerships.

Venus Square Nodes. In social situations, your emotional reactions are inappropriate. You're the proverbial fish swimming upstream against social norms.

Venus Square Ascendant. You're rarely satisfied with your close relationships or your marriage partner. You need to develop insight into your own motives and needs and strive to communicate those needs.

Venus Square Midheaven. Somehow, your career and home life always seem to conflict with your social and artistic needs and desires. Get rid of the chip on your shoulder, and strive to improve your behavioral patterns.

Venus Square Part of Fortune. Your romantic inclinations and financial habits can cause setbacks in your life.

Mars Squares

This aspect creates friction due to rash and impulsive speech and behavior. It also triggers intense and often focused activity and ambition as well as some sexual concerns. By seizing the energy of Mars and using it constructively, this square can be conquered.

Mars Square Jupiter. Slow down and don't count so heavily on your luck, because when it runs out, you'll be up against the consequences of your actions. Your life is screaming for moderation.

Mars Square Saturn. Your judgment is flawed. You either overestimate your abilities, your luck, or both. Lighten up on yourself, and control your temper. Go out and have some fun!

Mars Square Uranus. Your temper can be so explosive and fierce that it threatens to overtake your entire personality. Sudden, unpredictable events disrupt your plans. If you're not very careful, you can get seriously hurt, or even die from your throw-caution-to-the-wind attitude. Watch out!

Mars Square Neptune. This aspect is often found in the charts of astrologers and psychologists because it allows insight into deep, unconscious patterns. Your active imagination seeks expression through art, music, and dance, all of which are excellent vehicles for the mystical and psychic inclinations of this aspect.

Mars Escapism

Escapism—addiction to relieve stress and boredom—can be prevalent with Mars Square Neptune. It is highly recommended that those with this square focus on the more healthy practices in life and make sure to avoid alcohol, drugs, and even cults.

Mars Square Pluto. Your sex drive and aggression are pronounced. When something pushes one of your buttons, your temper can be explosive. When you refuse to acknowledge the friction of this square, it finds expression in some other area of your life, thus forcing you to change.

Mars Square Nodes. If you control your anger and get rid of your resentment, you're able to use the energy of Mars more constructively.

Mars Square Ascendant. You can't bully your way through life and expect to be viewed as a paragon of gentleness and diplomacy. You need to learn tact and cooperation or your partnerships and marriage will be filled with discord.

Mars Square Midheaven. You bring your work problems home with you, which creates disputes and arguments with your family. Stop being an agitator. Think before you speak.

Jupiter Squares

These squares are similar to those with the Part of Fortune. They tend to hinder the beneficial aspects of the planet.

Jupiter Square Saturn. Aim higher. Your goals are too limited, narrow, and restrictive. You would certainly benefit from workshops in self-confidence, visualization, and using your imagination to succeed.

Jupiter Square Uranus. You love to gamble in a big way with investments, real estate, or business deals. You would be better off curbing this impulse because you might lose your shirt. You're too impulsive.

Jupiter Square Neptune. Your wanderlust propels you into foreign countries: the more exotic, the better. If you were born into money, you won't hold onto it for long. To overcome the challenge of this square, you need to cultivate pragmatism.

Jupiter Square Pluto. You're dogmatic about religious and spiritual issues. Your beliefs are so inflexible that you have no tolerance for people who don't believe as you do.

Jupiter Square Nodes. Your religious beliefs and educational experiences aren't in step with the prevalent societal trends. Take steps to correct this, and your life in general will be much simpler and easier.

Jupiter Square Ascendant. People perceive you as bombastic and perhaps intellectually arrogant. You try to do too much at once and, consequently, end up doing few things well. Learn to focus on one thing at a time and cultivate humility.

Jupiter Square Midheaven and IC. You have a large family and a large home, both of which place heavy financial burdens on you. Strive to be realistic about your abilities.

Saturn Squares

Discipline, patience, and perseverance are the cornerstones of Saturn squares. The friction created isn't easy to deal with, but if you learn the lessons, tremendous inner strength and resilience result.

Saturn Square Uranus. Saturn imposes discipline, while Uranus screams for freedom. You're constantly confronted with situations that require thought and consideration, but the Uranian influence chafes at the restraints.

Balance!

With Saturn square Uranus, you're swimming against the current. Balance is necessary and will help you tremendously. Control your hot temper if you want to reap the benefits of your madcap creativity.

Saturn Square Neptune. Lack of ambition characterizes this square. It's not that you can't do what you set your mind to; it's simply that you don't feel like exerting yourself. Your best bet in overcoming this square is to find something that stirs your passions. Plan on how you can attain it, and go after it.

Saturn Square Pluto. Your hunger for power may be acute. You may be involved in schemes, plots, and intrigues—the stuff of spy novels. To conquer the friction of this square, you need to be brutally honest with yourself and attempt to change.

Saturn Square Nodes. Your selfishness and outdated prejudices hold back your development. Honest self-appraisal helps overcome the challenges of this square.

Saturn Square Ascendant. Others probably see you as somewhat aloof, maybe even cold. This is certainly true when strangers intrude on your time or people make unreasonable demands. Learn to structure your time so that your life is more balanced.

Saturn Square Midheaven. Your home life as a child was probably rigid and overly disciplined. As an adult, your responsibilities to your own family and parents may block or delay your career ambitions.

Uranus Squares

These squares affect generations of people. Their impact on personal horoscopes depends on whether Uranus is prevalent in the chart. Remember that Uranus deals with original thinkers and the outrageously unique.

Uranus Square Neptune. Think rebellion, pioneers, idealism, and psychic talent. The generation born under this aspect (1950s) faces tremendous social upheaval and emotional confusion. Their lives are disrupted by wars, catastrophes, and major disasters.

Uranus Square Pluto. Worldwide, this suggests upheaval, fanaticism, and massive destruction. The generations born under this aspect (1930s) are now in their seventies and eighties and have faced drastic social upheaval in their lives.

Change the Order of Things

On a personal level, with Uranus square Pluto there can be a need to reform and change the established order of things in general.

Uranus Square Nodes. You don't think much of traditions. You're a nonconformist at heart, but at times you take it so far you alienate the very people who could be helpful.

Uranus Square Ascendant. You want to be unpredictable and rebellious, but don't expect other people to love you for it. If you don't change, your intimate relationships aren't going to improve at all.

Uranus Square Midheaven and IC. You bounce around a lot by changing jobs and moving frequently. You're forever seeking the elusive job or relationship that won't restrict your personal freedom. Step back, detach, and honestly evaluate what you're doing and why.

Neptune Squares

Like the squares of the other slower-moving planets, Neptune squares affect generations and impact a personal chart primarily if Neptune figures prominently in the chart. Problems arise through idealism and seeing the harsh facts with rose-colored glasses, in order to avoid dealing with reality.

Neptune Square Pluto. This ugly aspect last occurred in the early 1800s and will roll around again in the twenty-first century. It indicates the breakdown of society and the general collapse of the old paradigms and belief systems.

Neptune Square Nodes. Cultivate practicality and bring your mystical daydreams back to Earth. Stop drifting and dig in your heels. Set goals. Forget drugs.

Node Squares

Node squares, themselves, act as distractions in whatever areas they affect. They often offer penetrating insights into issues we would rather avoid. With node squares, you tend to blame other people for the things that go wrong in your life. As soon as you understand that you create your own reality, that you are completely responsible for yourself, you'll be on the way toward vanquishing distractions.

Neptune Square Ascendant. You don't mean to be deceptive or unreliable, but you often are. As a result, you attract people who reflect these traits in yourself. Be more aware of what you say, what you promise, and how you act. Cultivate honesty in yourself. Don't take criticism so personally.

Neptune Square Midheaven and IC. Your professional and home lives are most likely in a constant state of confusion and turmoil. Find your passions and try to channel them more constructively.

Pluto Squares

With any Pluto aspect, go back to the root meaning of the planet: transformation—the collapse and end of the old and beginning of the new. This also deals with regeneration, rebirth, and tough lessons that need to be learned.

Pluto Square Nodes. By adjusting to the nuances of pop culture and current trends, you overcome the darker aspects of this square. Everything doesn't have to be a life or death issue.

Pluto Square Ascendant. You're too aggressive and demanding in your personal relationships. You would do better trying persuasion instead of coercion and force to get what you want.

Pluto Square Midheaven and IC. You rebel against all authority figures: parents, law enforcement officials, employers, and the government. You want to reinvent everything, to transform existing institutions. You need to reassess your life and evaluate where you're going.

SUN AND MOON SEXTILES AND TRINES

Signs of Talent

Sextiles—60-degree angles—symbolize ease and provide a buffer against instability. Trines—angles of 120 degrees—are similar but relate more to inner harmony and a state of equilibrium. Sextiles and trines to the Nodes, Ascendant, Midheaven, and **IC** are so similar that it makes sense to discuss them together. In this section, find out all you need to know about these intriguing aspects and how they affect you and your life.

Sun Sextiles and Trines

Sextiles to the Sun pinpoint areas in which your abilities can be expressed positively; they often represent opportunities. Trines to the Sun enhance self-expression and generally indicate harmony in the affairs associated with the planets that form the sextiles and trines.

Sun Sextile Moon. You get along well with people. Try to help them when you can, and they, in turn, will do the same for you. You're successful working with the public and have the communication skills to do it well.

Sun Trine Moon. You attempt to create the kind of harmony in your home that you knew in your childhood. At times, your life is so pleasant and generally happy that you're apathetic about doing something when you should be asserting yourself.

Sun Sextile Mars. You're one of those individuals with seemingly endless reserves of energy. Your creative ideas usually find expression in some form because you're forceful about achieving them. But you don't step on anyone else's toes to accomplish what you want.

Sun Trine Mars. Your physical vitality keeps you moving long after your competitors have gone to bed for the night. You may follow some sort of exercise program that maintains your stamina and bolsters your already considerable physical strength. Good leadership abilities come with this trine.

Sun Sextile Jupiter. You have high ideals, lofty aspirations, and numerous opportunities throughout your life to manifest what you want. Your self-expression usually comes through the house that Jupiter occupies.

Sun Trine Jupiter. Luck, optimism, and financial prosperity usually accompany this trine. You have tremendous creative potential, but you may not do much with it unless squares and oppositions in your chart create sufficient friction and tension.

Finances and Creativity

Well-known astrologer Grant Lewi made a classic remark about the aspect of Sun trine Jupiter: "No poet with this aspect ever starved in a garret or anywhere else, for that matter." In other words, financial luck and creativity go hand and hand with this aspect.

Sun Sextile Saturn. Your ambition won't ever exclude everything else in your life. You plan carefully, take your work seriously, and structure your life so that everything is judiciously balanced. You achieve through your own efforts.

Sun Trine Saturn. You have great self-confidence, abundant talent, and luck. Opportunities often come to you. Combined with a Moon/Mars conjunction, those opportunities either drop into your lap out of nowhere or you create them.

Sun Sextile Uranus. Your personality is charismatic, magnetic, and often forceful. You're deeply intuitive, which gives you valuable insight into other people.

Sun Trine Uranus. You're an original and progressive thinker whom other people want to know simply because you're so different. Things happen around you. Your perception of reality is broad and profound; you never lose sight of the larger picture.

Sun Sextile Neptune. Much of your inspiration rises from the deeper levels of your psyche and flows easily into your conscious thought. Your creativity is considerable and, with a little effort on your part, can flourish and bloom.

Sun Trine Neptune. If you aren't self-employed now, then you should take steps in that direction because you don't work well under others. You're very psychic. In fact, much of your knowledge comes to you this way even if you don't realize it.

Sun Sextile Pluto. Deep within, answers and information are available to you. Once you're able to access this profound level, you'll understand why your will is so powerful and how you can use it to achieve what you want.

Sun Trine Pluto. You're the person who brings friends and loved ones back from the brink of chaos. You help restore order to their lives. You would excel at any profession where you can do this for other people.

Sun Sextile or Trine Nodes. You do just fine in most circumstances, with most people. Conditions, overall, in your life are helpful to you. With very little effort, you overcome whatever holds you back.

Sun Sextile or Trine Ascendant. You don't have much of a problem expressing who you are. You're honest in your dealings with other people and don't tolerate dishonesty from others. Personal relationships are harmonious.

Sun Sextile or Trine Midheaven and IC. Your family is helpful to your professional ambitions and success. They support your efforts completely, which is part of why both your professional and domestic lives are so harmonious.

Why No Venus and Mercury Here?

The reason that Venus and Mercury are not listed in this section is that it is impossible for the Sun to form a sextile or trine with these planets. The reason is that both Venus and Mercury are too close to the Sun to make a sextile or trine.

Moon Sextiles and Trines

These aspects deal with the expression of emotion, early childhood, and your relationship with your mother and women in general. They also focus on the harmony within your own home, certain qualities of memory, and intuition.

Moon Sextile Mercury. Your memory is excellent. Your emotions and mind operate together in complete harmony. This aspect favors writers or others who use communication skills professionally and may also work out of their homes.

Moon Trine Mercury. You have a lot of common sense, and you're a quick learner. Your ability to recall past events is nothing short of remarkable, but you're not hung up in the past. You communicate well, especially with members of your family.

Moon Sextile Venus. You have abundant charm and a generous nature. Your artistic interests and inclinations are considerable. This also indicates fertility and a fulfilling, happy marriage.

Moon Trine Venus. Financial prosperity and an element of luck go along with this aspect. It indicates that you're charming, refined, and physically attractive. You're an optimist, love children, and want or have kids of your own. Harmonious marriage is indicated.

Moon Sextile Mars. You're an emotionally charged individual whose energy and vitality propel you through whatever needs to be done. You may flare up occasionally, particularly if you're provoked, but you generally don't hold grudges.

Moon Trine Mars. You have good control over your emotions and passions and a quick, sharp intellect. Your emotions and your mind are rarely at odds. Your self-confidence and ease with the public is impressive and helps you to achieve your ambitions.

Moon Sextile Jupiter. Your hunches and gut feelings about situations and people are usually right on target. You have an enormous storehouse of experiential knowledge and an excellent memory. You nearly always recognize the good in people.

Moon Trine Jupiter. Unconscious urges may prompt you toward foreign travel where you seek evidence of ancient cultures or your own past-life connections with these places. Your spiritual leanings, whether orthodox or unconventional, form an intricate part of your inner life.

Inspire Others

With Moon trine your Jupiter, your optimistic outlook and charitable nature may just inspire others to do great things. More good news: This aspect also usually indicates a happy, satisfying family life and financial prosperity.

Moon Sextile Saturn. Your patience and insight allow you to understand the inner workings of personal relationships. You're able to structure your unconscious feelings so that you work with them consciously, with awareness.

Moon Trine Saturn. You're reserved and cautious by nature, but you don't allow this to hold you back. You're loyal to your family and friends, who return that loyalty to you. You're able to structure your creative impulses into practical projects.

Moon Sextile Uranus. You embrace change and use it to your advantage. Your heightened intuition allows you to quickly grasp the intricate workings of any situation. You're different from other people, but that has never bothered you.

Moon Trine Uranus. Your magnetic personality attracts stimulating people. The past holds meaning for you only in terms of what you learned from it; the future interests you far more.

Moon Sextile Neptune. Your imagination and psychic ability are equally strong and fuel each other. This is an excellent aspect for fiction writers, physicians, and psychic healers. Your memory may be photographic.

Moon Trine Neptune. Expression in dance, art, music, theater, acting, and writing are particularly strong with this aspect. Your nature is fundamentally spiritual, imaginative, gentle, and compassionate.

Moon Sextile Pluto. Somehow, you're always able to regenerate yourself through your emotions. You draw on the deepest levels of your psyche to find the answers or create the opportunities you need whenever you need them.

Moon Trine Pluto. Your emotional intensity is well controlled and channeled constructively. You use it, consciously or unconsciously, to evolve spiritually. Others recognize this quality in you and gravitate toward you because of it.

Moon Sextile or Trine Nodes. Although you remember the injuries and losses of the past, they don't hold you back. You learned from them and embrace your future. Cultivate your inner voice.

Moon Sextile or Trine Ascendant. You're sensitive to criticism, but as you get older you begin to understand why. You have a good sense of the public pulse and take advantage of it. Your sensitivity to other people's feelings helps you to get along with just about anyone.

Moon Sextile or Trine Midheaven and IC. Pay attention to the synchronicities in your life; they'll guide you to the path of your greatest fulfillment. Women and family members are helpful to your career and support your professional ambitions.

PLANETARY SEXTILES AND TRINES

Innate Talents and Eases

While sextiles and trines can be considered together, many astrologers argue that sextiles are more important. Both generally point to a talent or innate skill, but sextiles are generally more obvious and noticeable. Trines often reflect talents that are so much a part of your nature that you don't think about them.

Mercury Sextiles and Trines

These aspects provide opportunities for intellectual development and communication skills. They're excellent for professional writers, speakers, and people in public relationships or politics.

Mercury Sextile or Trine Venus. You're gifted in both speech and writing and have refined artistic tastes. Your lively intellect and gentle nature instill your life and relationships with harmony. Mercury and Venus are never far enough away from each other to form a trine.

Mercury Sextile or Trine Mars. Mental energy is what you're about. You're decisive, intellectually quick and agile, and able to finish what you start. This aspect favors professional writers, sports strategists, and professional speakers or politicians.

Be Part of a Group

Actually, the aspect of Mercury sextile or trine Mars is good for anyone involved in organizations. You're good at becoming part of a unit. Strangely enough, many astrologers claim that people with this aspect usually follow some sort of exercise program with a high rate of success.

Mercury Sextile or Trine Jupiter. You respect the truth, whatever its guise. You're an unbiased individual with broad intellectual interests. You teach and are involved in publishing, writing, universities, or religious/spiritual organizations.

Mercury Sextile or Trine Saturn. You're intuitive but practical. Your mind is finely balanced, your thought processes are structured, and you have the discipline to create whatever it is you want out of life. So go for it.

Mercury Sextile or Trine Uranus. Your thinking is well beyond the scope of the present, but you're somehow able to bring your advanced ideas into the here and now and communicate them. Your intuition and psychic awareness are well developed.

Mercury Sextile or Trine Neptune. Your psychic ability fuses seamlessly with your imagination, allowing you access to deep spiritual realms. Poets sometimes have this aspect as do novelists, shamans, mystics, composers, and spiritual speakers.

Mercury Sextile or Trine Pluto. Words are your gift. You transform and regenerate yourself through your intellectual resources and communication skills. Your profound insight into the nature of reality allows you to achieve luminous success.

Mercury Sextile or Trine Nodes. You've earned an intellectual ease through efforts in other lives. In this life, you use these gifts to overcome any limitations or restrictions that hold you back.

Mercury Sextile or Trine Ascendant. Your wit and self-confidence attract friends and allies who reflect your intellectual interests. You work hard at expressing your creativity, and it's likely that if you persevere, you'll make money at it.

Mercury Sextile or Trine Midheaven and IC. The people you care about most understand exactly who you are and what you're trying to do. They support your professional ambitions and urge you to follow and achieve your dreams.

Mercury Sextile or Trine Part of Fortune. You achieve your greatest success by evolving intellectually.

Venus Sextiles and Trines

These aspects signify opportunities related to social, financial, artistic, and romantic issues. They also indicate expression in these areas, as well as artistic ability.

Venus Sextile or Trine Mars. You get along well with the opposite sex. A lot of energy goes into your creative pursuits. You may even work with your spouse or significant other in some sort of artistic endeavor or business.

Don't Let Money Rule You

People with their Venus sextile or trine their Mars enjoy making money almost as much as they enjoy spending it. In fact, this can be a big problem! Spending all the considerable money that they earn can be a huge downfall. Start stashing some of it away.

Venus Sextile or Trine Jupiter. This lucky financial aspect allows you to attract wealth and ample opportunities for making money. You're admired by your peers and recognized in some way for your artistic ability.

Venus Sextile or Trine Saturn. Your social activities revolve around your business concerns. You're thrifty about money, but not penurious, and have numerous business opportunities to increase your financial base.

Venus Sextile or Trine Uranus. You're very attractive to the opposite sex and get involved in a variety of stimulating romantic affairs. You benefit through involvement in groups, which may include e-mail news groups and online chat groups.

Venus Sextile or Trine Neptune. Compassion, artistic ability, and spiritual depth are indicated by this aspect. This aspect quite often suggests great wealth, especially when combined with any Venus or Mars conjunctions with Jupiter.

Venus Sextile or Trine Pluto. Love is your vehicle for transformation and regeneration. You listen to your intuition and follow its guidance, particularly in romantic issues. This aspect also is often indicative of an inheritance and of material benefits in general.

Venus Sextile or Trine Nodes. Through your social contacts, you find the opportunities you need when you need them. You're very conscious of proper social conduct and protocol, which allows you to overcome the restriction of the South Node.

Venus Sextile or Trine Ascendant. Your physical beauty is enhanced by innate grace and charm, particularly in a woman's horoscope. You probably have considerable musical or artistic talent.

Venus Sextile or Trine Midheaven and IC. Through your physical graces and social contacts, you further your ambitions. Your home reflects your personal harmony and beauty and is often a social meeting place

Venus Sextile or Trine Part of Fortune. Financial prosperity and recognition of some sort comes through your social contacts.

Mars Sextiles and Trines

These aspects help channel energy and drive in positive, constructive directions. The planets and houses that are aspected indicate the areas of development that are enhanced.

Mars Sextile or Trine Jupiter. Physical strength, a muscular body, and integrity are indicated by this aspect. Your optimism and enthusiasm infuse your ambitions and provide you with many opportunities to realize your dreams.

Mars Sextile or Trine Saturn. You're a relentless worker, particularly in the pursuit of your ambitions and dreams. You're able to structure your considerable energy and creative ability to achieve what you want.

Mars Sextile or Trine Uranus. Your courage and daring extend to all areas of your life. In your profession, you don't hesitate to try progressive but unproved methods to attain results. Once you reach one goal, you embark on a new journey with new goals.

The Explorer

With this aspect, in your personal life, you're an explorer in the truest sense of the word. In other words, the need to explore affects your sex life and your need to travel.

Mars Sextile or Trine Neptune. You're compassionate, gentle, and blessed with spiritual insight. Your acute psychic ability alerts you to opportunities in finances and the arts that enhance your professional ambitions. You're secretive but honest.

Mars Sextile or Trine Pluto. Your enormously powerful will can bring about immense and drastic change in your life through which you evolve spiritually. Your insight into deep mysteries about the nature of reality is keen and profound.

Mars Sextile or Trine Nodes. Your timing is usually on target. This aspect favors politicians and celebrities whose lives are public. Your dynamic personality attracts people who aid you in your endeavors.

Mars Sextile or Trine Ascendant. Your directness impresses other people and makes them willing to help you. You're physically strong and your health is good.

Mars Sextile or Trine Midheaven and IC. You have numerous opportunities to advance yourself professionally. Your career is solid and dynamic and so is your home life.

Mars Sextile or Trine Part of Fortune. Your drive to achieve pays off because your ambitions are directed, funneled, singular. Your physical stamina and health are generally strengthened with this aspect.

Jupiter Sextiles and Trines

These aspects usually imply success and prosperity in the areas governed by Jupiter: law, publishing, religion and spiritual issues, higher education, foreign travel and cultures. The trines in particular are like built-in safeguards that mitigate other less fortunate aspects to Jupiter.

Jupiter Sextile or Trine Uranus. Your insight is highly developed and alerts you when to seize opportunities that other people miss. You travel suddenly and unexpectedly and have unusual experiences abroad that expand your perceptions of what is possible.

Liberal and Unconventional

Those with Jupiter sextile or trine Uranus usually have defined views of the world. Their political beliefs lean toward the very liberal. Their spiritual inclinations, too, are more unconventional and metaphysical rather than the orthodox and conservative.

Jupiter Sextile or Trine Neptune. This mystical aspect often finds expression in spiritual studies and attainment. Spiritual practices like yoga and meditation may be followed.

Jupiter Sextile or Trine Pluto. This is one instance in which the darker attributes of Pluto are absent. Your tremendous willpower and finely honed psychic ability indicate that you can emerge as a spiritual leader. You act on your spiritual convictions and are capable of instigating the kind of change that affects the masses.

Jupiter Sextile or Trine Nodes. Whatever direction your life takes is in keeping with your soul's intent. You have opportunities to correct the excesses or mistakes in past lives.

Jupiter Sextile or Trine Ascendant. This aspect attracts the things we all seek: good luck and health, happy marriages, and prosperous partnerships. Your optimism and humor attract loyal friends and supporters.

Jupiter Sextile or Trine Midheaven and IC. This is another one of those incredible aspects that indicates outstanding professional success and a happy domestic life. If you've got this aspect, consider yourself blessed.

Jupiter Sextile or Trine Part of Fortune. This aspect suggests material benefits, spiritual insight, and happiness according to the sign and house placements.

Saturn Sextiles and Trines

Considering the nature of Saturn, these aspects to the planet are always welcome. They enable you to structure your energy around realistic and practical goals, bring stability to your life, and often result in tangible rewards.

Saturn Sextile or Trine Uranus. The unique inventiveness and brilliance of Uranus is molded into practical expression by Saturn. You respect conventional thought, but aren't limited by it. You have an acute sense of timing.

Saturn Sextile or Trine Neptune. The dreamy, imaginative, and spiritual qualities of Neptune are brought down to Earth with this aspect. You're able to put your spiritual knowledge into action through humanitarian efforts on a small or large scale.

Saturn Sextile or Trine Pluto. Your ambitions are tempered by your innate understanding that if you're to effect change, you must do it through careful planning. It's quite likely that if you adhere to your path, you'll achieve a prominent and power position in your life.

Saturn Sextile or Trine Nodes. Your efforts are rarely without purpose. You find the proper vehicle for their most practical expression and, in doing so, overcome the limitations of your South Node.

Saturn Sextile or Trine Ascendant. You possess a quiet dignity that impresses everyone you meet. Any partnership you enter is usually beneficial to your long-range goals.

Saturn Sextile or Trine Midheaven and IC. You attain professional success through hard work and careful planning. Your home life is satisfying and orderly.

Saturn Sextile or Trine Part of Fortune. This aspect brings status, success, and good fortune.

Uranus Sextiles and Trines

If you're quick, if you're prepared, you'll be able to take advantage of the opportunities that show up with this aspect. Think of them as psychic gifts, things you've earned from previous lives.

Uranus Sextile or Trine Neptune. If Uranus or Neptune is prominent in your horoscope, then you're most likely spiritually aware. You're probably very psychic, with a mystical imagination that connects you to the deeper levels of reality.

Uranus Sextile or Trine Pluto. Under this aspect, great forces are harnessed and channeled. You abhor social injustice and strive to live your own life free of bias with your sight on the future.

Uranus Sextile or Trine Nodes. By following your path of humanitarian ideals and progressive thought, you evolve spiritually.

Uranus Sextile or Trine Ascendant. You're one of those magnetic personalities who attracts the unusual and often bizarre. You set trends and are constantly moving forward. You probably marry quite suddenly, and your significant other is as unusual as you are.

Uranus Sextile or Trine Midheaven and IC. You're not interested in following the crowd; instead, people tend to follow you because of your uniqueness. Your home is unusual in some way, with many interesting people coming and going.

Find Fame

People with Uranus sextile or trine the Midheaven and **IC** may just be in for a big surprise—fame. Though they're mostly not interested in all the attention they get, those with this aspect tend to become famous overnight.

Neptune Sextiles and Trines

These aspects emphasize imagination, artistic and psychic ability, and spiritual evolution. They affect large numbers of people.

Neptune Sextile or Trine Pluto. The personal importance of this aspect depends on the prominence of Neptune or Pluto in the horoscope. If either planet is placed in the first house, rules the Ascendant, or displaces the ruler of the chart, the Sun, or the Moon, then this aspect suggests intense spiritual evolution is possible.

Neptune Sextile or Trine Nodes. Your uncanny instincts about social trends put you in the professional driver's seat. Your spiritual pursuits allow you to evolve and overcome the limitations of the South Node.

Neptune Sextile or Trine Ascendant. This aspect favors marriages and partnerships. You're compassionate, sympathetic, and idealistic and have a mysterious allure that attracts the good will of others. You feel psychically attuned and connected to your mate.

Neptune Sextile or Trine Midheaven and IC. You use your intuition in your profession to alert you to opportunities. You share a psychic connection with your parents, a significant other, and close family members.

Neptune Sextile or Trine Part of Fortune. Intuition is a major factor in your life. Use it to recognize opportunities and to manifest what you desire.

Pluto Sextiles and Trines

If Pluto is strong or prominent in your chart, then these aspects are definitely good ones to have on your side.

Pluto Sextile or Trine Nodes. Your intuition is well developed and one of your most valuable assets. It allows you to see past appearances to the truth of a situation. You have the ability to influence how others think on a broad scale.

Pluto Sextile or Trine Ascendant. Your willpower and natural clairvoyance give you a decided edge on your competition. You're able to raise the level of consciousness in other people and are presented with many opportunities to increase your personal power.

Pluto Sextile or Trine Midheaven and IC. Your career opportunities are many and varied. Through them you gain professional prominence and power. Your intuition helps you to direct your career and overcome any obstacles or challenges in your domestic life.

SUN AND MOON OPPOSITIONS

180 Degrees Apart

Oppositions are as easy to spot in a chart as conjunctions are. They lie directly across from each other. Planets in the first house, for example, are in opposition to planets in the seventh house. Oppositions involve conflict and tension. They often represent our own personal attributes that we project onto others.

Sun Oppositions

Tension is the basic nature of an opposition. To overcome it, you have to reach a compromise. With Sun oppositions, the tensions manifest as a conflict of wills. Note that no opposition exists between the Sun and Mercury and the Sun and Venus.

Sun Opposed Moon. Your emotions are pitted against your ego. The stress may show up in your relationships with the opposite sex. It can also affect your health, especially in a woman's horoscope. By understanding the nature of the aspect, you go a long way toward overcoming it.

Sun Opposed Mars. When people disagree with you, take a dozen deep breaths and remove yourself temporarily from the situation. This will ultimately get more results than your usual hostile reactions.

Sun Opposed Jupiter. Your inflated ego and grandiose schemes don't exactly endear you to others. Learn to listen sincerely to other people, and you can mitigate the influence of this opposition.

Sun Opposed Saturn. You chafe and rebel against the restrictions imposed on you by others. These restrictions may come from heavy responsibilities you take on for a spouse, parent, or child. This aspect asks that you attempt to take all things in stride.

Sun Opposed Uranus. The bottom line is that you can't have everything your way all the time. Your insistence on this, coupled with your extreme independence, makes it difficult for you to get along with other people. Until you clear up this dichotomy in your life, expect a lot of tension with friends and partners.

Sun Opposed Neptune. Meeting the challenge of this aspect requires strength of will and great focus. You're easily deceived by other people and confused about your religious beliefs and personal relationships. Strive for objectivity.

Sun Opposed Pluto. Your overbearing nature can get on other people's nerves. Many people are intimidated by the forcefulness of your personality, so you tend to lose support you might have otherwise.

Sun Opposed North Node, Conjunct South Node. Vanquish your selfishness and learn to cooperate with other people. Look to the houses occupied by the Sun and the Nodes to determine which areas will be affected.

Sun Opposed Ascendant. This aspect means the Sun is also conjunct the seventh house cusp. This focuses energy on marriages and partnerships. These intimate relationships fulfill and ground you. They provide you with the self-confidence to assume leadership roles.

Sun Opposed Midheaven, Conjunct IC. Your professional achievements are largely dependent on the harmony of your domestic life. You need a fulfilling home life to be able to function well in the larger world.

Moon Oppositions

This aspect creates tension and conflict in your emotional nature. You may have trouble relating to others on an emotional level and are always very aware that you need to develop in the areas influenced by the Moon opposition.

Moon Opposed Mercury. You talk too much about nothing, have trouble finding the proper words to express your opinions and thoughts, and have difficulty relating to people emotionally. As a result, you're indecisive and frustrated.

Moon Opposed Venus. You sometimes erect emotional walls to protect yourself. This creates distance between you and the people you love and causes unnecessary problems.

Needing Love

Since Venus relates to feminine power, Moon opposed Venus may indicate feelings of not getting the love you want from your mother or a mother-like figure. Extravagance may also be directly related to these early instances of hurt childhood feelings.

Moon Opposed Mars. You're wired too tightly emotionally. This causes impulsiveness and makes you impatient, restless, and volatile. There can be some dislike for women in general.

Moon Opposed Jupiter. You're much too emotional. You waste a lot of energy fretting about small things in your life. Step back from your emotions.

Moon Opposed Saturn. You withdraw emotionally to protect yourself from other people. This creates problems with other people, who may see you as somewhat inhibited, even cold. Your professional ambitions drive you.

Moon Opposed Uranus. The emotional connection with this aspect often originates in an insecure childhood. You shy away from restrictive emotional ties of any sort, move frequently, and your relationships with others begin and end abruptly.

Moon Opposed Neptune. You're a psychic sponge who absorbs the emotions and attitudes of the people around you. You tend to project your own emotional confusion onto other people, which makes it difficult in your relationships to determine who is feeling what.

Negative Energy

With Moon opposed Neptune, you're prone to negative energy—in fact, your body shows it. Any health problems you have now may just stem from early childhood experiences and belief patterns. Work these things out.

Moon Opposed Pluto. Your conflicts with others revolve around joint finances and inheritances. Step back and honestly assess where you are in your life and where you would like to be five years from now. Then implement a plan to get there.

Moon Opposed North Node, Conjunct South Node. The belief patterns that hold you back originated in early childhood and are deeply immersed in your psychological makeup. If you work at breaking these patterns, do so gently.

Moon Opposed Ascendant. You have excellent insight into the needs and wants of the public, which benefits you professionally. Most of the time, you prefer the company of others to solitude; you find emotional fulfillment through others.

Moon Opposed Midheaven, Conjunct IC. You're close to your parents and have warm memories of your early childhood. The death of a parent can result in deep shock. You don't like being away from your family and may not take jobs that cause you to be away from them for any length of time.

PLANETARY OPPOSITIONS
Tension and Balance

Keep in mind that oppositions, although they include tension and antagonism, can also mean balance. People often focus on the first feature to the detriment of the second. There are positive solutions to even the most intractable-seeming opposition.

Mercury Oppositions

This aspect creates enormous tension in your communication with others. Heated disagreements often occur, usually because of intellectual beliefs you hold.

Mercury Opposed Mars. You're intolerant of other people's ideas that differ from your own. You argue about everything, and when you can't win an argument, you resort to shouting. Your behavior is often crude and hostile, even when you don't mean it to be.

Cultivate Patience

Those with their Mercury opposed their Mars need to cultivate patience and less aggression—the need to dominate and be right. Get rid of the chip on your shoulder and detach from your emotions when dealing with others. Work on your ability to listen and understand before you speak.

Mercury Opposed Jupiter. You tend to blame others for your own failures. But the truth is that your grand plans and ideas lack practicality, and you usually promise more than you can deliver. You need to cultivate responsibility for yourself and your own actions.

Mercury Opposed Saturn. You're bright, you have ability, and you're an excellent listener. But you fret too much over inconsequential details and throw up blocks that impede the natural flow of ideas. Lighten up on yourself and be more patient.

Mercury Opposed Uranus. In all probability, you're a genius. But your ideas may be too eccentric to be practical. Your complete indifference to other people's opinions often results in bad timing. You should nurture an interest in other people and try to bring your genius down to earth.

Mercury Opposed Neptune. You're very sensitive to other people's feelings, but sometimes you can't seem to help what you do or say to them. You hate being pinned down in any way, so instead of saying yes or no to something you simply refuse to commit. This produces chaos.

Mercury Opposed Pluto. You're very good at organizing secretive or sensitive information and have an innate understanding of opposing views. Your language, however, sometimes borders on the obscene, which offends others.

Mercury Opposed North Node, Conjunct South Node. You need to keep learning and not settle with the knowledge that you already have. Through education and intellectual growth, you overcome the limitations of the South Node.

Mercury Opposed Ascendant. Since this aspect means that Mercury is conjunct the seventh house cusp, it indicates a solid mental rapport with significant others. You may attract a younger lover or spouse.

Mercury Opposed Midheaven, Conjunct IC. Your home is loaded with books and other intellectual materials. You have a good rapport with your family, even though they may not always support your professional ambitions.

Venus Oppositions

This aspect usually suggests conflict in the romantic and social arena. This can mean challenges in marriages and partnerships, artistic expression, and financial matters.

Venus Opposed Mars. For a woman with Venus more dominant in the horoscope, it implies that you may leave yourself open for abusive relationships. If Mars is dominant, you may be sexually aggressive and act without consideration for anyone else's feelings.

Venus Opposed Jupiter. Your insincerity toward others shows up as grandiose gestures toward strangers and people you barely know. As a result, most of your relationships are superficial.

Venus Opposed Saturn. It's difficult for you to reach out to others emotionally. You may be shy and withdrawn with the opposite sex. To overcome this challenge, you need to get in touch with your emotions.

Venus Opposed Uranus. Emotionally, your need for personal freedom is constantly at odds with your need for companionship and stimulation. You need to find balance in your relationships and within yourself.

Venus Opposed Neptune. Your idealized notions about love, romance, and money prevent you from seeing things as they are. Your expectations are unrealistic.

Venus Opposed Pluto. You need to be more aware of the motives for your actions. Are you trying to remake your significant other rather than working on yourself or your own beliefs? What parts of yourself are you projecting onto others?

Venus Opposed North Node, Conjunct South Node. The problem in overcoming this aspect is that you get pleasure out of your habitual patterns regarding relationships and finances. Unless you seriously scrutinize these patterns and attempt to change them, it will be very difficult to overcome the restrictions of the South Node.

Venus Opposed Ascendant. Since this aspect means that Venus is conjunct the seventh-house cusp, it indicates happiness and success in marriage and partnerships. You derive much pleasure and happiness through your personal relationships.

Venus Opposed Midheaven, Conjunct IC. Your deepest pleasure comes through your home life. Look for aspects to the tenth house that may create harmony or conflict with ambition goals because of your attachment to home and family.

Mars Oppositions

This aspect infuses a horoscope with aggression, energy, and anger. Your reaction to sensitive issues is likely to be rash, impulsive, and hostile. If other adverse aspects to Mars are present, you may experience physical danger.

Mars Opposed Jupiter. Scrutinize your own motives in the way you treat other people. Are you being friendly or gracious just to get something out of them? Your restlessness and thirst for adventure send you off on trips to foreign countries.

Mars Opposed Saturn. These two planets are really at odds. Mars wants to rush ahead impulsively; Saturn wants to plan. You're frustrated and angry much of the time and resent others whose lives seem to be clicking along smoothly. Try to go out of your way to help others.

Mars Opposed Uranus. You either work to the point of exhaustion or are consumed by laziness. Your explosions of temper are followed by remorse. Step back, chill out, and seek balance.

Mars Opposed Neptune. You're better off avoiding alcohol, drugs, sexual excesses, and clandestine activities of any sort. Make great efforts not to lie, cheat, or act in an underhanded way. Above all, examine your own motives.

Mars Opposed Pluto. Your personal desires are at war with your higher or spiritual self. In the charts of self-aware people, this aspect tests what you're made of: Do you bow to your personal desires or do you follow a higher path?

A Good Example of Mars Opposed Pluto

The conflict of personal desire with spiritual self here is a lot like the struggle between Darth Vader and Luke Skywalker, especially once Luke knows that Darth Vader is his father. Luke must decide to kill or to connect with Darth Vader. In this way, he's caught in an internal battle with himself.

Mars Opposed North Node, Conjunct South Node. If you learn to control your flagrant disregard for social conventions and traditions, you'll break the restrictions and limitations that hold you back.

Mars Opposed Ascendant. A lot of energy goes into your close partnerships. Your confidence attracts dynamic partners whose ambitions match your own. Friction that arises may have to do with who calls the shots.

Mars Opposed Midheaven, Conjunct IC. Your home life may be riddled with arguments and disagreements. Your responsibilities toward your family may interfere with your career ambitions. Balance is key. Cultivate it.

Jupiter Oppositions

This aspect creates conflict in terms of expansion, religious and spiritual issues, higher education, the law, and any of the other affairs ruled by Jupiter.

Jupiter Opposed Saturn. Professional success may be gradual with this aspect, but your perseverance and dedication make it happen. The negative parts of this aspect are greatly mitigated by trines, sextiles, and conjunctions to Saturn.

Core Beliefs Determine Reality

Always remember that your core beliefs determine your reality; the patterns in your horoscope merely reflect what is possible. If you cultivate and maintain optimism, even when faced with enormous challenges in this aspect, you will stay well ahead of the game.

Jupiter Opposed Uranus. In a chart that lacks direction and focus, this aspect may lead to involvement with revolutionary groups who do little more than make trouble and break rules. You may be prone to a purposeless wanderlust and flights of imagination that have no grounding in reality.

Jupiter Opposed Neptune. Spiritual conflicts sometimes come up with this aspect. Illusory thinking and utopian ideals fail to find practical outlets unless there are positive aspects to Saturn. Cultivate pragmatism and look beyond the mask that other people present to the world.

Jupiter Opposed Pluto. Your religious and spiritual convictions are an intrinsic part of your life. Unfortunately, you try to convert everyone to your way of thinking about these issues and create considerable animosity.

Jupiter Opposed North Node, Conjunct South Node. You get a lot of pleasure out of your excesses, even though they're actually impeding your development. Work to develop yourself through the house placement of the North Node.

Jupiter Opposed Ascendant. Since this means that Jupiter is conjunct the seventh-house cusp, it indicates good fortune generally in marriage and partnerships. Your significant other supports your ambitions, and you benefit through the cooperation of others.

Jupiter Opposed Midheaven, Conjunct IC. Your family's generosity embraces all areas of your life. They fully support your professional and personal endeavors. Your spiritual beliefs are strongly influenced by your parents.

Saturn Oppositions

With this aspect, look for conflicts concerning tradition, authority, discipline, structure, and anything that Saturn stands for.

Saturn Opposed Uranus. These two planets are locked in combat. They represent totally opposite traits. Discipline and structure are pitted against freedom and reform. Even though you demand total freedom from others, you tend to be dictatorial toward other people.

Saturn Opposed Neptune. Your sense of reality may be seriously flawed. You need to step back from your life and take a long, hard look at what you're doing and where you're going. Instead of using subterfuge to deal with people, attempt to cultivate directness.

Saturn Opposed Pluto. If you're up to the task of personal evolution, this aspect helps you do it, but only through hard work and discipline. It's a good idea to study this aspect in light of the rest of the chart. If criminal tendencies appear elsewhere, this aspect can confirm it.

Saturn Opposed North Node, Conjunct South Node. To evolve, you need to break with tradition and convention. Try the new; seek out the unconventional.

Saturn Opposed Ascendant. This aspect indicates a solid marriage and partnerships. You may marry later in life or to someone older than you. You shoulder your part of the overall responsibility.

Saturn Opposed Midheaven, Conjunct IC. Your childhood was probably far too strict and your early life, too rigid. You feel a heavy duty to your parents and/or family, and this feeling inhibits and frustrates your career ambitions.

Uranus Oppositions

This aspect tends to bring about traumatic experiences that cause shattering disruptions and irresolute change. Once the pieces fall, you have to rebuild. The success or failure of your transition is entirely up to you. If you rise to the challenge, you succeed.

Uranus Opposed Neptune. On a broad, societal scale, this aspect causes major disasters, upheaval, and turmoil. On a personal level, if either planet rules or is prominent in your chart, it creates deception and delusion related to the houses Uranus and Neptune occupy.

Uranus Opposed Pluto. In a generational sense, this aspect causes sweeping and destructive changes in society. If Uranus or Pluto prevail in your chart, this aspect indicates sweeping and often violent changes in your life.

Uranus Opposed North Node, Conjunct South Node. You should temper your eccentric attitudes and try to go with the prevailing social flow. Even if it seems to block your personal freedom, it will do more for your freedom in the long run.

Uranus Opposed Ascendant. Your partnerships, romantic and otherwise, tend to happen suddenly. The partners you attract are exciting and unusual. Even if the relationships don't last long, it's a great adventure.

Love Is Liberating

When you're ready for stability in a relationship, try not to worry so much about your personal freedom. You may discover that love—real love—can also be incredibly liberating.

Uranus Opposed Midheaven, Conjunct IC. You need to be your own boss and call your own shots. Your hunger for personal freedom seems to interfere with everything else in your life.

Neptune Oppositions

Even when Neptune is badly aspected, it's not all bad. Its better attributes—psychic ability, imagination, artistic talent—remain. The problem with the oppositions is that they create enormous tension and conflict between ideals and the reality.

Neptune Opposed Pluto. This one comes down to the archetypal struggle between good and evil, destruction and regeneration. It last occurred in the early 1800s and will come around again in the twenty-first century.

A Realignment—Good or Bad

At its worst, Neptune opposed Pluto suggests an era of psychic and spiritual depravity, when sexual perversion and debauchery are the norm. On the other hand, within the rubble of changed old belief systems, a spiritual alignment can take place that revolutionizes the way we perceive reality—for good.

Neptune Opposed North Node, Conjunct South Node. Your habits are so ingrained that you may not even recognize them as habits. But unless you break them, you fail to evolve to your potential.

Neptune Opposed Ascendant. Relationships are your blind spot, but you can be just as deceptive as the people you get involved with. Your intuitive ability is so finely tuned it can give you the inside track on whatever you focus on.

Neptune Opposed Midheaven, Conjunct IC. You may have an unstable home life where psychic abilities are the norm rather than the exception. Good. Take it for its worth, then head out into the world on your own and satisfy your spiritual hunger.

Pluto Oppositions

Think of the marriage vow: for better or for worse. That's the nature of all aspects to Pluto, but this is particularly true in the case of oppositions.

Pluto Opposed North Node, Conjunct South Node. This aspect is all about the Western view of karma. Old debts need to be repaid before you can progress or evolve through the area indicated by the house placement of the North Node.

Pluto Opposed Ascendant. Relationships and partnerships may not be entirely pleasant for you. Get rid of your need to dominate, keep your spiritual self uplifted, and the influence will be diminished considerably.

Pluto Opposed Midheaven, Conjunct IC. Much of your inner life will wrestle with the issue of spiritual evolvement. You may get sidetracked. One way or another, the events and conditions in your life bring you back to the bottom line: Get it right this time around or you'll be back to try again.

CHAPTER 7

PRACTICAL ASTROLOGY

Astrology can often seem like an endless stream of charts, symbols, and numbers. It's true that astrologers spend an awful lot of time looking things up in charts, consulting notations about the positions of various heavenly bodies, and so on. All of this is necessary in what has become, over the centuries, a very complicated system.

However, all this is directed toward very practical ends. Astrological studies can help your love life, your financial well-being, and your health. People often consult astrologers when they're considering some large change in their lives (moving to a different city, changing jobs, ending or starting a relationship, and so on). In all of these areas, astrology can play a role in helping you toward the right decision.

In the Middle Ages and up through the Renaissance, rulers often maintained court astrologers to advise them regarding political and military matters. The most famous of these, discussed earlier, was Elizabeth I's court astrologer John Dee, but there were many others. We no longer use astrologers in matters of national political import (although Nancy Reagan reportedly passed along the comments of her astrologer to her husband Ronald). Still, in everyday practical affairs, you may want to consider consulting a professional astrologer. In this chapter, we'll look at astrology's advice in matters of love, health, and finance.

LOVE: FIRE

Aries, Leo, and Sagittarius

Love compatibility is a tricky thing. On the one hand, there are so many obvious matches, but some supposed mismatches work, too. It's difficult to know everything from a couple's set of Sun signs. However, Sun signs will give you a basic idea of whether or not you'll get along as a couple.

Aries in Love

Aries man has a penchant for doing things his way. He's as sharp as a tack and people respect him, even though they think he's bossy and domineering. He'll decide how he wants it done, and he's a perfectionist about it. If he likes you, he'll listen to your take on it, and perhaps tailor it a bit. But if he doesn't like you, watch out! He must win every argument—even when he's wrong.

Avoid Jealousy

Never get too jealous with Aries man or Aries woman. They both hate it. They need to know that they can do whatever it is they want to do. If you're too jealous, they'll run out and start a fling, just to prove that they're in charge.

Aries woman, on the other hand, handles people with more charm and finesse. She's a lot less aggressive than Aries man—on the outside—though her thought process is very similar. Where he drives forward, she'll pull back and wait for the masses to come to her—and they always do. When it comes to love, she's just as fickle and stubborn as Aries man.

Seduction Tips with Aries

You won't have a problem seducing Aries if he likes you—both the female and male gender of this sign are easily stirred and definitely not shy.

- Resist a little and let him work for it. You'll have Aries intrigued and more excited about the encounter.
- Don't count on words alone. Aries is a wordsmith and sometimes better at talking about the deed and thrilling you with words than he is at actually performing the action. He's bigger on promises and idealistic futures than on living up to his seemingly fluent words of love and the future.

Change the Rules Frequently

With Aries, take everything with a grain of salt, and you'll be ahead of the game. They always want what they cannot have. With Aries, you have to change the rules frequently, or they'll get bored.

Aries, unfortunately, can woo you into bed with well-placed words. Whether or not he can accomplish the tasks at hand depends on each Aries. Aries is confident—too confident in bed. And he's sensitive, too. He might tell you about his own downfalls, but he'll absolutely freak out if you start listing them.

Aries can be a bit selfish in bed, too. Sure, he's creative, exciting, and extremely inventive. He thinks he's sensitive but he's not necessarily— unless his Venus is in Taurus, Cancer, or Pisces. If his Venus is in Aquarius or Aries, beware! He can woo you to the ends of the earth, but he can also be detached. You'll believe you know him, and then he'll change right before your eyes.

Tips

- Go slow with Aries and make her work for it.
- Never put her on a pedestal—treat her as an equal.
- Praise her only when she deserves it. Make her listen to you but understand that she'll only see her side of it. Accept this.
- Don't ever try to control her, or she'll run the other way.
- Give her freedom but also set boundaries.

Matches with Aries

If you want a faithful Aries, try to stay away from those who have their Venus (their love sign) in Aries, Sagittarius, or even Aquarius. They tend to wander. If you're an Earth sign, pick an Aries with lots of Air in his chart—he'll be drawn to you. If you're a Water sign, you'll probably do well with Aries if he has a lot of Fire.

And if you want an Aries who lives for love, find an Aries with his Venus in Cancer or Pisces. Aries, because it's a Fire sign, is often attracted to other Fire signs—Sagittarius or Leo. But generally, unless aspects in the chart indicate otherwise, romance with another Fire sign can be explosive. Aries gets along well with Air signs—Gemini, Libra, Aquarius—or a sign that's sextile (60 degrees) or trine (120 degrees) from Aries. Sometimes, an Earth sign helps ground all that Aries energy. In chart comparisons, a Venus or Moon in Aries in the other person's chart would indicate compatibility.

Leo in Love

Leos are passionate. They can also be impulsive and irrational, but it's all part of the charm. They're fickle, and they like to test their partners before they put their hearts into anything. They're difficult, too, particularly when their egos need to be stroked. If you treat a Leo with anything but the ultimate respect, he may not say anything, but he'll remember it—and count it against you in the game of love.

Confidence Can Be an Act

Though Leo gives the appearance of being confident and secure, this is often an act. Leo's innermost desire is to be accepted for who he is, and his biggest worry is that he'll soon discover he's just normal or boring. It's very important for a Leo to feel special.

Leo fights for the underdog, but be sure to stick up for yourself with him. On the other hand, arguing for the sake of arguing will make a Leo insane. Leos are intense and will argue, but their sunny, calm natures are truly made for being content and feeling safe and comfortable with a partner.

If you make a Leo feel secure, he'll be more likely to fall in love with you. However, making him secure doesn't mean making yourself a doormat. Let Leo know he can be himself with you—that you won't judge him—and he'll relax in your presence and show his true colors.

For the most part, Leos need to feel needed and need to know they are loved before they commit entirely. Once they're committed, everything is bigger than life and brighter than the Sun. They're known to be loyal, but this is only true after they've found themselves. If they haven't, and they're not yet emotionally evolved or secure, they can be as two-faced as Gemini can be.

R-E-S-P-E-C-T

Like all Fire signs, Leo needs to respect you in order to fall in love. This means that you need to be ambitious in career, straightforward in your dealings with people, and truthful with them.

Many astrologers say Leos are arrogant, but this is not true. Actually, they're such perfectionists that they're worried their insecurities will show unless they "perform." They show off sometimes and try to be larger than life to compensate for their flaws.

Seduction Tips with Leo

Courtship is often a series of dramatic gestures: five dozen roses that arrive at your office, an erotic call at 3:00 a.m., or a chopper ride over Manhattan. It's the truth—Leo is a big spender—or, at least, he has big ideas about luxury in life.

- One thing that is sure to turn off a Leo forever is pettiness. If you're petty in any way—asking for money for something big or small (that should be water under the bridge) or being vindictive with a friend or family member—Leo will be annoyed and leave you in the dust.
- Don't be frugal. Leo simply can't tolerate paying for things he doesn't deem worthy. True, he understands the difference between paying for a $300 hotel and a $500 hotel; but if you'd prefer to stay in a mud hut with no air conditioning or heat, you'd better find another Sun sign to do it with.

Leos Aren't Good Liars

If you're involved with a Leo, make sure you know his intentions with you. Ask him. He'll tell you. Leo is not a very good liar. If you ask him in person, chances are that you'll get the truth from him. (Or you'll at least read it in his facial expressions—pay attention!)

Leo needs to believe that it's his idea to give a relationship a chance. If you push too hard, you'll scare him off. He likes to win—always likes a prize. You need to be the prize he wins. Leo won't mind putting up a fight for you. There needs to be a fine line, though. If you make Leo work too hard, he'll just walk away.

Deep down, Leo wants everything but isn't quite sure he's really worthy. Therefore, Leo must feel special, yet not fawned upon (until he's in love, and then it's fine). Finding a perfect balance is essential in order to gain Leo's trust and affection.

Matches with Leo

Another Fire sign is good for a Leo simply because their energy levels are similar. Any sign that is sextile (Gemini, for instance) or trine (Aries) would be fine, too—though Leo has little patience for Aries who aren't spiritually evolved. True, he may win her for a while, but then what? He can be too headstrong. Aries is a lot like Sagittarius with Leo— lots of fire, but not the same temperament. Sagittarius can be a bit too wise and quiet (or even too superficial or stubborn) for Leo; Aries can be too demanding and controlling.

The polarity between Leo and Aquarius, its polar opposite sign, may elevate a Leo's consciousness to where it succeeds best—to the wider world beyond himself, if the Leo has some Air signs in his chart. Capricorn can be an interesting match and Scorpio seems like a go until Leo realizes that she may not like the way he may raise their children. But they're surely a good match in bed.

Sagittarius in Love

Exotic places, individual searches for truth . . . these are Sagittarian themes. No matter who a Sagittarian loves or marries, a part of him or her is always slightly separate and singular—aware of the larger picture.

No Disrespect

The surest way to get rid of a Sagittarius is to disrespect his words. You must listen to everything he says—Sagittarius is very big on authority. He is. Heed Sagittarius' "lectures" and he'll appreciate you for it.

Sagittarius is pretty clear in what he wants. He knows if he's in love. It's simply not a question. "Making" a Sagittarius fall in love is difficult. You can play a little hard to get in the beginning, and this will help, but, ultimately, Sagittarius is instinctive and wise—and knows what he needs.

He's so blunt and tactless with his words that they can sometimes cut to the core. But believe everything that comes out of Sagittarius' mouth. If he tells you he's in love, he is. If he tells you he's not, he's not. Sagittarius is not a very diplomatic soul. In his mind, honesty and straightforwardness is everything, and he likes someone who will listen carefully to everything he has to say.

Strangely enough, Sagittarius sometimes gives the impression that he's lost in another world. He seems quiet—or into himself. This isn't entirely true. It always seems that Sagittarius is deeper than he really is. In truth, he's probably thinking about work or some kind of problem in quantum physics—he's not thinking about your relationship.

Sagittarius wants everything to go smoothly. In his mind, if things are not moving forward, he's not going to waste his precious time devoting it to you. Just don't badger him for his thoughts. Let Sagittarius come to you to ask you how you're feeling. He needs to be left alone to experience his space and freedom, and then he'll come search you out.

Seduction Tips with Sagittarius
If you keep Sagittarius guessing, you'll keep him.

- Be direct with your words, and quieter with your emotions. Sagittarius likes to be steered in love in a very subtle way. He's very physical and sometimes expresses his feelings through actions, rather than through words.
- Never be needy with a Sagittarius. He'll be out the door faster than you can blink.
- Sagittarius is also one sign that will absolutely do what you tell him not to do. Don't even try it. Instead, try using reverse psychology. Say, "Oh, you're right ... you're so right ... but maybe just this once, could we try it this way—just for me?"
- Don't ask for too much in the beginning. He'll give you his heart—and everything else—if you don't ask for a lot right away. He needs to be "there" in the moment with you.

Sagittarius is very capable of separating sex and love. If he's sleeping with you, it doesn't necessarily mean he's in love. Again, you need to ask him what's going on. Don't do it in a needy way. Ask him in a direct way—he'll tell you. Just remember to believe what he says. Sagittarius doesn't mince words.

He's more sensitive than he seems, and he'll care for anyone he gets involved with. As passionate Fire signs go, Sagittarius is a good guy—and he's even better when he's in love. Just make sure not to lie to him. Sagittarius won't appreciate that at all. If he doesn't trust you, he'll be nice to you, but he'll run the other way looking for a better mate.

Matches with Sagittarius

Other Air signs are compatible with Sagittarius. The Sagittarius-Gemini polarity confers a natural affinity between the two signs. But other Fire signs might work well, too. It just depends. Sagittarius, above all other Fire signs, is the most emotionally secure. Sagittarius is not the most stable (Leo is), but he thinks he is. This can make him a bit of a know-it-all. He doesn't tolerate as much as Leo, but he's not as ridiculously immature as Aries can sometimes be.

He comes off as a natural, quiet leader. And he is. The best match for Sagittarius is a Water sign—particularly Pisces. These two go together so well because Pisces is strong and sensual enough for Sagittarius, but is also a master in the art of silent persuasion. Sagittarius needs someone who is loving, sweet, and tender, will let him do what he feels like doing, and isn't nitpicky about the little things. Again, a Water sign might just do him good because he likes being "shown the way"; yet, all the while, he's the one who can act "in charge" of things.

Least Faithful, Most Faithful

When Sagittarius falls in love with The One, she's set for life. Sagittarius can be the least faithful sign of the zodiac, but she can also be the most faithful. If she finds what she's looking for, Sagittarius will settle down and not look any further.

In essence, you can get a Sagittarius to fall in love with you if you are sweet, yet strong. He hates being argued with; so, if he does something stupid, approach him in that moment and just tell him what he's done wrong. He won't put up with silent passive-aggressive tactics. These drive him crazy (though once in a while these will keep him on his toes). He doesn't go for the shy, sensitive type, though. He needs to feel that his mate can do fine without him. Only then will he stay.

LOVE: AIR

Gemini, Libra, and Aquarius

Air sign compatibility is tough to discern. They're so quick and mentally agile, and they like to stir things up. They're all havoc-seekers on some level. Libra does it quietly; Gemini is a drama queen and a gossip; and Aquarius is hard to pin down. But all Air signs will give a relationship that extra uncertainty factor.

Gemini in Love

The problem with Gemini is that he doesn't really know what he wants. He thinks he knows, but then it changes. Gemini needs to work for love—then he'll give his all. Also, he needs a partner who makes him laugh—but not about himself. Geminis can be touchy and sensitive when the humor comes at their expense.

Geminis love first with their minds. Even a relationship that begins primarily because of a sexual attraction won't last if there's no mental connection. Quite often, Geminis seek friendship first with the opposite sex and, once a mental rapport is established, the friendship deepens into love. But this happens when they're really ready for something serious. Otherwise, they can have affairs like no other sign in the zodiac.

When It's Over, It's Over

Once Gemini is over you, it's really over. Don't ever take a "break" with Gemini—it won't ever come back around to the way it was. Gemini has this power to cut it off clean and never look back once he's decided it's through.

Geminis have a "need to try everything once" attitude. True, there are some Geminis who won't sleep with a person if they're not in love, but chances are, they'll try it all with the one they're with at the moment.

Again, Geminis give great advice, though they're just not very good at taking the advice, themselves. So, they're a little lost. And they change their minds frequently, so it's sometimes difficult for them to get to the heart of the matter. All of that aside, Geminis do love with every bit of their hearts. They're pretty quick to put their hearts on the table when they feel it—sometimes too quickly. They can be diplomatic when they need to—but not when it comes to romance, love, and you.

Seduction Tips with Gemini

Gemini is the biggest flirt in the zodiac. He'll flirt in front of you, and has charm like no one else (except maybe Libra), but this is all part of the game. Sure, he can be faithful—you have to win his heart first. Unfortunately, this isn't an easy task. Gemini will always go for the "coolest" person in the room, unless he's looking to settle down for real. Then, he may go for the perfect person who grounds him.

Winning the Prize

Gemini needs to feel like he's got the prize that other people covet. In other words, it's not just okay that he thinks you're great, he needs to know that his friends think you're amazing, too. So, don't hang on him at parties. Show that you're independent but that you're on his side.

- If you have a head for business or simply a good job, this will impress Gemini to the umpteenth degree. He wants to respect his partner and know that his partner has big ambitions.

- Geminis know that sarcasm and humor with an edge is the best remedy for everything. Make a Gemini laugh—at himself and at others, in general—and he'll instantly think you're smart.
- Never go against Gemini in front of his friends. He'll be instantly offended and look elsewhere for romantic company

Gemini really does need a little drama to know that you're interested, but he doesn't like being alone for long. He can get caught up with his work for a while, but work will never be the most important thing in his life—not deep down. Love is the real focus. In fact, he'll stay with someone he thinks is the best thing he can find around. And if you stay on top, for him, he'll be with you—always.

Matches with Gemini

Geminis are social enough to get along with and be attracted to just about anyone on a superficial basis. They feel most at home with other Air signs, particularly Aquarians, whose minds are as quick as theirs. They also get along with Sagittarius, their polar opposites in the zodiac, who share some of the same attributes. Again, though, these are broad generalizations. For compatibility purposes, it's important to compare the individual charts.

When Gemini is ready to settle down, an Earth sign may be a good option for a partner. A Virgo will be a bit too critical for the thin-skinned Gemini, but a Taurus, with his feisty sensual side, may just be what the doctor ordered. Capricorn can go either way, but most Capricorns won't put up with Gemini's otherwise flighty antics or superficial skimming of political ideas that hold great truths for Capricorns.

Again, an Air sign like Libra may be ideal for Gemini if they can find a balance of minds. If anyone can find that rare balance, it's Libra. The only problem is that Libra despises confrontation and Gemini tends to go that way. Water signs are probably too side-stepping for feisty Gemini—unless they have a lot of Earth or Air in their charts. Scorpio and Gemini are a good match in bed, but Scorpio sometimes weighs Gemini down when he wants to go out and play. Leo can be a fun dating partner for Gemini—with a lot of laughter—but Leo may get annoyed when Gemini doesn't praise the ground she walks on. If Gemini does, it's a match made in heaven.

Libra in Love

Libras are drawn to beauty, whatever its form. The only thing they enjoy as much as beauty is harmony. Even when a relationship has gone sour, a Libra hesitates to be the one who ends it. Libras can't stand hurting anyone's feelings. As a result, they may remain in a relationship longer than they should just because disharmony is so distasteful. Libras seek harmony because, in their hearts, they know that enlightenment lies at the calm dead center of the storm.

In fact, Libra is just that—the eye of the storm. Libra is the ultimate "watcher" of human behavior. He studies it—studies you—and determines what he knows and what he believes, from that. He'll have his friends study you and see if you're faithful and "worthy." Ultimately, he'll make up his own mind. But if a Libra doesn't trust you, you're history. He'll never put the time in to get to know you.

Find Out What Libras Want

Libra has a very fixed idea in his head of what he's looking for. If you don't fit that perfect mold, he's not going to waste his time on you. Find out what Libra wants. If you don't, you may seduce him for one night, but he won't get serious with you.

It seems as if Libra has many friends. True, he has a wonderful social circle and many people who believe in him. But watch closely. Libra keeps his true self hidden from the world. There's usually only one person he truly trusts—usually a family member. If he opens up to you completely on a consistent basis, you've got a real mate for life.

Librans are masters in the disguise of their own fate. It's sometimes difficult for them to make a tough decision, but when they do, no one can talk them out of it. Librans believe in signs, red flags, and even superstitions. They'll consider omens and apply them to their own lives.

Also, Librans want to be calm and comfortable in a relationship. Many Libra men choose younger women just to have this feeling of ultimate control. Sometimes they also pick women a lot older than they are so that the woman does all of the deciding. You'll also find that Librans are mostly faithful when they find the one they want to spend time with. True, they may have strange arrangements set up, but when they love, they love deeply.

Seduction Tips with Libra

With Libra, you must first determine if he's learned to cope with emotional feelings. Many Librans can be immature—they like to push sentimentalities away in an attempt to rationalize them. They're Air signs, after all. But they can also be overwhelmingly idealistic and sensitive. So, it takes a Libra a bit longer to get to know himself (and show himself). All the while, it may be difficult for a partner to deal with this constant back-and-forth of letting himself go and reining himself in.

- Libra likes to feel in control. In this way, you may have to be demure in the beginning.
- Let Libra chase you. Don't let his friends know that you're interested. Libra will get the hint just by looking at you in the eyes. His eyes

are the key to his soul. In fact, that's how you'll know that a Libra is interested. You'll feel it in your gut.

- Libras are very sensitive, so try not to make the first move. Because of the internal battle all Libras must face, they like to have a little bit of dominance in the situation. And they tend to judge a mate unfairly if she's too aggressive.

- Let Libra man steer the conversation and the relationship. Pull back, at first, and let him court you. He'll do it in a grand way, and you'll be glad you did.

Matches with Libra

Librans can get along with just about anyone. They are most compatible with other Air signs, Aquarius and Gemini. Though seriously outgoing, Geminis can sometimes scare them—they understand the way Librans think. Scorpios get to the heart of the matter with Libra; they have the intensity and emotional depth that Librans crave. In fact, Librans might even get attached to Scorpios in a volatile and unhealthy way, if they're not careful. Though Scorpios can be a good match for Libras, they should watch out for signs of control. If Librans feel they're being manipulated in any way, they'll be out the door in a flash.

Librans also gravitate toward people who reflect their refined tastes and aesthetic leanings, like Leo. Also, an Earth sign may provide a certain grounding that a Libran needs. Taurus is a wonderful, sensual match with Libra. Or a Water sign, like Cancer, may offer a fluidity of emotion that a Libran may lack. But, with Cancer, it may be an uphill battle. Cancers can be too moody, sometimes, and too self-involved for harmony-seeking Librans.

Since opposites attract, Aries can sometimes be a good fit for Librans—though Aries needs to have spiritually "found herself" before this can work. On another note, a Libra with a Libra can be a good match—but watch out! Two of the same signs together can be wonderful or a big mess.

Look for Your Best Side

When you pick someone of the same Sun sign as you, it will magnify all of your good traits—and your bad ones, too. It's like looking in the mirror. Do you like what you see? Or does it bring up issues for you? Always choose a partner who brings out your best side.

Aquarius in Love

Aquarians need the same space and freedom in a relationship that they crave in every other area of their lives. Even when they commit, the need doesn't evaporate. They must follow the dictates of their individuality above all else. This stubbornness can work against them if they aren't careful. Aquarians usually are attracted to people who are unusual or eccentric in some way.

Aquarians can be very instinctive but usually for other people, not for themselves. They also root for the underdog, but sometimes pick the wrong underdog or victim to defend. Their upbeat, positive outlook on life can be tempered by idealistic notions they try hard to suppress. The biggest goal in life, for them, is to remain calm and cool. This is very important for Aquarius because, when they let loose, they can be fireballs. If they get too wound up, the aggression they exude can be harsh for other people to cope with. Instinctively, they know this and try to temper it, often unsuccessfully.

Aquarians know that they're strong individuals and that they can turn the tides to their favor. Luck follows them everywhere—even if they're not aware of it. They may even sense where they're headed before the fact. An Aquarius is not a big mystery, though. If you want an answer about love, just ask. Aquarians will tell you if your relationship is headed somewhere or not. If they're not sure, chances are that the answer is no, but they can be swayed over time.

Survivors

Aquarians are survivors—know this. So, if you want to be with one, know that they're hardheaded with their decisions. Under that cool exterior is a person who must, eventually, follow their heart and mind. And this can be difficult, too, because the two forces don't always agree! But sticking around with an Aquarius will pay off. They'll trust you and slowly get attached.

Aquarius also must see a bit of the world before settling down. He may even get married a couple of times before realizing that he just wasn't ready for what he thought he was. An ideal partner for Aquarius will show his own mental agility, his independence, and his emotional strength of will. This will get an Aquarius to follow you to the ends of the earth, but only if he's ready for something real to enter his life.

Seduction Tips with Aquarius

Aquarius tests people to see how smart and cool they'll be when they realize they've been had. If someone overreacts or is too sensitive to this test, Aquarius will lose interest. It's all part of being fascinating, interesting, and fun for Aquarius. He has to know you'll play the mental games he loves to play—and that you're strong enough to handle them. Therefore, don't get angry when Aquarius tests you. Laugh about it—and do it back. Aquarius will appreciate this!

- Unlike some other signs, Aquarius is impressed with bold, aggressive moves. You can grab an Aquarius when you want and he certainly won't shy away. Just make sure you have the mental connection first, or you'll be wasting your time.
- Aquarians are capable of having sex or a fling without getting emotionally connected at all. They won't judge you if you sleep with them right away, usually, but if you get overly romantic or clingy when Aquarius isn't quite as into it as you are, Aquarius will back away from the situation.
- If an Aquarius has a short fling, or encounter, it doesn't mean their hearts will be in it. Aquarians can turn their emotions on and off, but only when they're not in love. When they're in love, it's another story altogether. What will keep an Aquarius going is challenge. Like Aries, Aquarius always needs a challenge on some level in all of their relationships—or they won't take you seriously. Remember, Aquarius is a survivor and knows that nothing worth having comes too easily.

Matches with Aquarius

Due to the lack of prejudice in this sign, Aquarians usually get along with just about everyone. They're particularly attracted to people with whom they share an intellectual camaraderie—someone who makes them laugh and makes them feel good about themselves. In this way, Gemini can be a fabulous match for Aquarius, as long as they don't butt heads. This relationship can work only if the two find balance between neediness and independence. Also, Gemini can be extremely jealous and possessive with mates, which Aquarius abhors.

Many Aquarians wind up with Virgos. Virgos have the kind of stubbornness and organized stability that Aquarians secretly crave. But this may also be an ego-thing. Remember, Aquarius loves a challenge and Virgo keeps them squirming with their moral lectures and hardheaded ways. But, mentally and in bed, these two can do very well together.

Aries and Aquarius

Aries is usually a good match for Aquarius. Together, they have lively, fascinating conversations, plenty of spunk, and mental camaraderie. Unfortunately, the flakiness factor of Aries can be evident to Aquarius, and he's not sure if he can trust her. However, he likes the challenge.

A Libra or another Aquarius can be a good match—especially if one is more outgoing and gregarious than the other and lets his partner shine. Aquarians are usually secure enough to see bad and good traits in a partner that are similar to their own, and still be able to deal with it and move ahead with the relationship.

A sign that's sextile or trine to Aquarius will also work. Aquarius's polar opposite, Leo, can be an interesting mate for Aquarius. If Aquarius doesn't get too self-involved and gives Leo her fair due, this can work. But Leo is usually running after Aquarius, and Aquarius can get bored of that—fast. If Leo pulls away a little, this rapport can function well. All in all, Aquarius is a great partner if you've truly won his heart. If not, you'll just be a stop along the way for lively Aquarius, who craves adventure and experience.

LOVE: WATER

Cancer, Scorpio, and Pisces

Water signs in love are the craftiest and most manipulative of all the signs. But they get away with it because they're very special. However, try wronging a Water sign like Pisces, Cancer, or Scorpio, and you'll be sorry. They have a way of pushing your buttons, getting to the heart of the matter, and forcing you to fall all over yourself to accommodate them. They're "feeling" signs, like Fire, but they have patient endurance that the Fire signs lack, allowing them to win in the end.

Cancer in Love

Cancers can be evasive when it comes to romance. They flirt coyly, yet all the while they're feeling their way through the maze of their own emotions. Cancers feel deeply; they're also very good at putting their feelings "on hold." In other words, if they're not already in love with you, they can pull back and see the relationship for what it is at a distance.

On the other hand, if they're in love, it's not so easy for them to let go. They tend to go the cheating route to push away a partner rather than fess up and just say how they feel. In fact, beware of Cancers dodging questions and important issues. They find it difficult to open up and talk about their true, personal feelings. If they do, with you, you've got an edge over all the others. Once again the whole "side-stepping" part of Cancer is absolutely true. True to their crab sign, they mimic the crustacean with surprising accuracy.

Getting to the Heart of Things

Some Cancers dislike the courtship of romance altogether and prefer to get right down to the important questions: Are we compatible? Do we love each other? The problem is, they tend to go through this by themselves or with a very close friend—not with you. Be direct and ask what's going on.

They enjoy entertaining at home because it's where they feel most comfortable, surrounded by all that's familiar to them. They feel comfortable around water, too. From the fluidity and calmness of water springs their vivid, fantastical imaginations. Cancers are "idea" people—and can truly explain any strange, unusual, or outrageous concept to you.

Just remember: to live with and love a Cancer, you have to accept the intensity of their emotions. It's a war they have within themselves, and they'll want to embroil you in it. Unfortunately, they're too busy taking care of you and others to know (and show) what's eating at them. You'll have to get to the heart of the matter yourself.

Seduction Tips with Cancer

There's one thing that many astrologers don't tell you: Cancers are like Geminis in that they love to laugh. They're usually funny, themselves—though either in a biting or subtly ironic way. But here's the thing: Geminis like making people laugh even more than they appreciate others who make them laugh. Cancer is the opposite.

- One way to win a Cancer is to show him you two have the same sense of intelligent, dark humor. In fact, if you don't make a Cancer laugh, chances are that he'll have a hard time falling in love with you.

- Cancer men tend to go for only three types of women: the victim, the wild (fire sign) card, or the good girl—in that order. When they're younger, they'll fall for someone who needs to rest on their shoulders. However, when they realize that a partner won't reciprocate, they'll get sick of it and walk away. Later on in life, they'll go for all kinds of women—especially the "wild card," whom they can't control. However, this is not a good match for them and they'll see it clearly, eventually. But they like a little drama, even if they despise confrontation. Cancer men, many times, will date women who are older than them—or much younger. Or both.

Perhaps the worst thing you can do with a Cancer is to take everything too literally. If you don't understand the idea of "concept" and the subtleties of grand schemes, forget Cancer. Cancer is good at seeing the big picture. They stall at the idea of future and forever-after, but they'll know, deep down, when they get there. Cancers don't have to be faithful at all but, once they make the wedding type of commitment, they're bound to be settled for good.

Play Along

Cancers like to poke and prod. They like to make fun—and will do it just to get your goat. Don't let them get the best of you. Play along! If you act too touchy if they joke with you, they'll think you're too rigid.

Matches with Cancer

On the surface, Pisces, as the other dreamy Water sign, would seem to be the most compatible with a Cancer. But Pisces's all-over-the-map sense of style with Cancer's sidestepping can be frustrating for both.

As well, the duality of Pisces would, most likely, drive a Cancer person crazy. One of the best combinations here is Water sign, Scorpio. Cancer manages Scorpio with bravado and knows how to get the ever-changing Scorpio hooked. A little mystery goes a long way with Scorpio, and, in the case of this match, Cancer cannot help but induce a little intrigue with her onslaught of bottled-up emotions that just lie beneath the surface. Scorpio might just bring it out of Cancer.

Earth signs—Taurus, Virgo, and Capricorn—are particularly good for Cancers with Taurus and Virgo because they are sextile to Cancer. Fire signs with Cancer, on the other hand, tend to bring out the worst in Cancer—unless it's, perhaps, a very evolved fire sign. In rare cases, Leos do well with Cancers (especially if the Leo is the man).

Scorpio in Love

You don't know the meaning of the word intensity unless you've been involved with a Scorpio. No other sign brings such raw power to life. The rawness probably isn't something you understand or even like very much, but there's no question that it's intricately woven through the fabric of your relationship.

It's never obvious how the intensity is going to manifest: jealousy, fury, endless questions, or soft and intriguing, but effective passion. Sometimes, the intensity doesn't have anything to do with the relationship, but with the personal dramas in the Scorpio's life. Many times, you may even hear from work colleagues that he's a "perfectionist, and difficult to work with."

Scorpios have a magnetism that is legendary. It doesn't even matter if he's good-looking—it's always there. Scorpio is always the sexiest person in the room, known for his bedroom prowess. Unfortunately, other problems can weigh Scorpio down so he's got to be clear of mind and calm in order to woo you in his cool, mysterious way.

Speaking of mysterious: there's something with Scorpio that you may just not be able to put your finger on. If he's completely direct with you, that's good. Chances are, though, he's got a number of secrets he keeps hidden from the world. It may be something that's happened in his past, or a fetish he doesn't want to let you in on, or even another woman he sees occasionally. Beware.

Obviously Lying

You'll always be able to tell when Scorpio is fibbing. You can feel it. The energy around him changes. If you keep insisting that he tell you the truth, he may even get angry. The only way to get the truth out of him is to get him in a good mood, pretend you don't really care, and then get him to confess.

Scorpio's senses are strong, especially those of sight, touch, and taste. If he touches you, you'll feel it down to your toes. He has keen sight, meaning instincts. If he cooks, he's wonderful. If not, he appreciates everything about food. However, there's one sense he lacks: hearing. It seems as if he doesn't hear anything you say. It's not that he doesn't really remember. Instead, he has a mental block on the things he doesn't want to remember, or he's very likely to pretend he doesn't know what you're talking about. The truth is, Scorpios have excellent memories. Don't let him get away with this.

Seduction Tips with Scorpio

Scorpio man needs to woo his woman. Do not chase after him. He may do it subtly, at first, but eventually he'll invite you for a weekend away somewhere special. Scorpio has a knack for finding a romantic way to court (and win) a partner. Scorpio is also relentless in his pursuit of a mate, and usually gets what he wants.

- He likes very sexy, yet tasteful. He'll negatively judge a potential mate if the sexy part extends to flirting with his friends—don't do it.

- Scorpio might keep his rage hidden for a while, but it won't work in your favor to make him over-the-top jealous. He'll just think you're not the good girl he thought. Scorpios will have flings with too-sexy women, but they will never marry them.

- Many Scorpios are hidden workaholics. They're very good, in the beginning, at hiding this fact. This is why: They need to complete a task before they can go on to the next. Therefore, the thing that will be most important for a Scorpio is to "get you," and then, predictably, he can go back to his normal routine of working crazy hours, complaining about it, and never resolving the problem.

- Many Scorpios have obsessive tendencies—whether or not you see them in the beginning. Truth is, at first it may just seem like you're the obsession. He'll be so bent on getting you that you'll wonder if you've just stepped into a romance novel. Be aware that this may change, later. Scorpio can't leave the duties of his job for long—he defines himself by it.

- Know, too, that if he's having many problems at work, your relationship will suffer. He needs to resolve work issues before he can think of getting intimate again. He absolutely cannot separate these two parts of his life—try as he does. In this respect, you must understand and be supportive. There's no other way around it.

In the case of Scorpio, before you even think of letting romance get the best of you, you must determine if you're getting involved with someone who can handle a real relationship. Many Scorpios are perfectionists, with work and with themselves, so ask yourself: Is this person happy with his life? In other words, does he constantly say "poor me"? The thing is, if a Scorpio is not happy, deep down, he will go into periods of self-doubt and pity—and will bring you down with him. Some

Scorpios are emotionally mature and can handle the world around him. Find out first, though.

Don't Chase

Scorpio will stay in a romantic situation that's not working for longer than he should. If he starts pulling away a little, or is less jealous or possessive than he was before, you're probably losing him. The worst thing that you can do at this point is to chase after him. Be busy, pull away, and let him come after you. Scorpio is a lonely, private soul—but he absolutely hates being alone, too.

The best time to approach a Scorpio about something important is after lovemaking. His guard is let down almost completely. Be aware of Scorpio's temper. He bottles things up inside and then it all comes out at once—in a huff. Don't ever try to convince Scorpio the he is wrong at this point. Let him calm down first. If not, he'll never see your side of it.

Matches with Scorpio

Scorpio is usually compatible with Taurus, because the signs are polar opposites and balance each other. The Water of Scorpio and the Earth of Taurus mix well. However, both signs are fixed, which means that in a disagreement neither will give in to the other. Scorpios can be compatible with other Scorpios as long as each person understands the other's intensity and passions. Pisces and Cancer, the other two Water signs, may be too weak for Scorpio's intensity, unless a comparison of natal charts indicates otherwise.

Fire signs may blend well with Scorpio, depending on their charts. If a Scorpio is emotionally solid, a Leo may be a good match. Scorpio loves Leo's sunny nature, and is drawn to it. If Scorpio doesn't pull Leo down with him, this can work. Sagittarius, especially if Scorpio is near the cusp of Sagittarius, can be the same—but ditto with the "bringing her down with the house." If the two can respect each other and find a good balance, this can work. Aries and Scorpio, however, will find that the emotional gap is probably too much of a chasm to cross.

Pisces in Love

Through the heart, sensitive Pisces experiences his subjective reality as real, solid, perhaps even more tangible than the external world. For some Pisces, romance can be the point of transcendence—the source where he penetrates to the larger mysteries that have concerned him most of his life. To be romantically involved with a Pisces is to be introduced to many levels of consciousness and awareness. If you're not up to it, then get out now because your Pisces isn't going to change.

There is nothing weak about Pisces. Instead, Pisces watches from a distance and determines the best point of attack. Pisces, also, many times seems the quiet type, who's sweet and kind. But when Pisces is in a relationship, and feels comfortable, there is no one who can manipulate you and your feelings like Pisces can (except, maybe, Cancer). The way a Pisces does this is to play cold and walk away until you follow. Pisces knows that this always works in human nature and has this move down to a science.

He's strong because he'll get you to come to him without any effort on his part. Pisces are ten times craftier than they appear. They're incredibly good at hiding this side of them. They're so adept at playing along with you, and being "on your side," that you won't even know what hit you when they use something—something you've told them—against you, in the future.

Pisces is idealistic. Pisces is also a dreamer but not impractical about it. Most Pisces know what they want and go after it with a kind of slow, methodical gait. Eventually, most of them get what they want, even if it takes time. But Pisces instinctively know how best to get the most out of their astonishingly calm composure and patience.

Can You Pass the Test?

Pisces will test you. All Pisces know how to test and how to get the answer they're looking for at the moment. If you're smart enough, you'll recognize this and pass the test. If not, Pisces will turn away without warning and find someone worthier of his affections.

Pisces includes a little bit of every sign and can usually pull out this grab bag of talents at will. He can be a little mysterious like Scorpio, play the noble like Leo, insert the commanding attitude like Sagittarius, be the charmer like Gemini, and act the part of smooth-talker like Aries. The only role that Pisces has difficulty playing is Aquarius, whose sign sits right next to Pisces.

In fact, Pisces have a hard time hiding disdain for those they don't like while Aquarius is perfectly capable of fraternizing with the enemy, if need be. And Aquarius does not turn up his nose at anyone, while Pisces does so often. Pisces has a regal Air about him like Leo. While Leo is more of the caring, noble set, Pisces has a proud, capable, and studious air about him, which, try as he may, he cannot shake.

Sympathetic and Empathetic

Pisces is intelligent and empathetic. Don't ever confuse sympathetic with empathetic, though. Pisces will not feel your particular brand of sadness, though he seems to. Instead, he's likely to bring you out of the despair by "understanding" your plight and giving you good advice for it. But the sadness he shows you will never reach his heart.

However, there is no one like Pisces to give you good advice. Aries may be good at it, but he orders you around while doing so. His words are more command and "truth," than suggestion. Gemini is good at it, but usually comes up with the overly aggressive way. Instead, Pisces will put the idea into your head and let you come up with the solution. This is, indeed, most effective and one of Pisces's best traits.

Seduction Tips with Pisces

Pisces, in love, would do anything for his mate. If he's not in love, though, he can look at the relationship with astonishing coldness (even if he finds it difficult to break away). Pisces, like Cancer, has a tough time deciding what he truly wants. There's something always in the back of a Pisces's mind that says "I could probably do better." And, because of Pisces's idealism, he'll always wonder what kind of mate he'd have in a perfect world. Also, in all likelihood, he could make you a list of how he imagines this "perfection."

- Pisces has a thing for power. If you're someone he can look up to and admire, you'll win Pisces's heart for sure. Unlike the Air signs, Libra, Gemini, and Aquarius, Pisces will be more won over with accomplishment and quiet romantic gestures than by pure physical beauty.
- Since Pisces likes the cool and understated, your manners, gestures, and even dress should be tasteful and elegant, not showy or ostentatious, ever. Again, the way someone puts herself together will be more important to Pisces than makeup or any other superficial marks of anything but natural, regal beauty.
- Pisces appreciate directness and fire—gumption and energy. They love intensity and romance, in a grounded and refined way.

Matches with Pisces

Other Water signs seem the obvious choice here. But Scorpio might overpower Pisces and Cancer might be too clingy. The signs sextile to Pisces are Capricorn and Taurus. While Capricorn might be too limited and grounded for the Piscean imagination, Taurus probably fits right in. Gemini, also, because it's a mutable sign like Pisces, can be compatible.

The real shocker here is that Sagittarius may just be the best combination for Pisces. Though they're such opposites, they complement each other quite well. Pisces is able to soothe the Sagittarius savage beast—and they fit like two pieces of a puzzle. Pisces also lets Sagittarius do what he wants, yet always keeps the upper hand with a cool, polished, quietly strong demeanor. And this is what Sagittarius likes best. As for the other Fire signs, there doesn't seem to be much chance, but it truly depends on the other factors in the two separate charts.

LOVE: EARTH

Taurus, Virgo, and Capricorn

In love, Earth signs can fall hard, but they'll struggle and protest along the way. They're ten times more sensitive than people think they are—only because they don't necessarily wear their hearts on their sleeves. For Earth signs, most things are black and white, and love is no exception. Earth signs are known to be stubborn, but when they love, they love truly and deeply.

Taurus in Love

In romance with a Taurus, a lot goes on beneath the surface. Taureans are subtle and quiet about what they feel. Once they fall, though, they fall hard. In fact, their inherent fixed natures simply won't allow them to give up. Taurus people get in way over their heads and then find that there's no turning back.

However, a Taurus will never really fall in love unless he thinks he can trust you. Trust goes a long way with Taurus. Deep down, Taurus knows that he's sensitive and that he takes himself a little too seriously. His sense of responsibility weighs heavily on his shoulders and he'll always fulfill any task he believes he must.

But, remember: he'll also feel like it's up to him to judge the world. If he's critical, take it as a warning. He definitely has an idea in his head of how things should be, and he'll try to mold you into how he sees you or how he'd like to see you. Pay close attention to his naggings because, though it may seem otherwise, he means every word he says.

As a Venus-ruled sign, Taureans are true sensualists and romantic lovers. Their romantic attachments ground and stabilize them. Love is like air to them: They need it to breathe. Again, they'll want to trust and rely on you. This is essential. In fact, it's very easy to see if Taurus trusts you, at least to some degree. Taurus can't touch and make love unless he feels he can. Taurus and Virgo may be the only men in the zodiac who are mainly like this. They might entertain a fling or two in their lifetime, but that's not what they're about.

Instead, they're looking for meaning and true love—someone who'll put up with their obstinate nature and even revel in it. Most Taurus men are macho. Like the bull, they're quite direct and will usually take a problem on—head on (quite the opposite of the way Cancer would handle it). Give them a good love challenge and they won't shy away. Taurus is built for competition. The problem is, he may never really stop to consider if you two are actually good for one another.

Talk Things Out

Unlike most other signs, Taurus should not be dealt with on a physical level when the two of you fight. In other words, you'll probably need to talk things out before you make love again. Remember, Taurus is sensitive and puts his heart into lovemaking. Don't try to make up with him with kisses.

Seduction Tips with Taurus

Taurus women (and sometimes men) have a habit of falling for Fire signs. In the beginning, the Fire sign will conquer her. But once she starts getting comfortable, he begins flirting with others and testing her. If she lightens up, she just may be able to keep him.

- Never make a Taurus too jealous. He'll punish you for it and get revenge. Sure, he'll do it quietly and methodically, but it will come back to you.

- Taurus men like the slow art of seduction. Never go to bed with a Taurus too quickly. He'll never respect you for it. Taurus wants to make love, not just have sex, and it's a slow, seductive tango. Taurus definitely doesn't rush. If you're not into languid, sensual lovemaking, a Taurus may not be for you. Even if Taurus likes to talk "dirty," he still wants to know that the feelings there are real. Then he'll be able to loosen up and be himself in bed.

- Deal with issues as they come up. Don't go to bed angry. Work out your problems. Taurus is good at dealing with the issues at hand. Instead, if he pushes them deeper and deeper, you will never get them out of him again. When you bring it up, he'll look at you like he has no idea what you're talking about—even if he's steaming inside. Instead, he'll talk about it years from now when you least expect it.

- Taurus is capable of holding a grudge for decades. It's very difficult for him to let go of the past. He remembers everything and never forgets anything. Try to be direct and honest with Taurus all the time. Don't let him get on a self-pity track. It's his self-defense and armor. If a partner from his past has wronged him, he'll look for every conceivable reason that you'll do the same to him.

- Find out where he's sensitive and make sure you stay far away from that route. In other words, if an ex cheated on him, go out of your way to show him that you're more than trustworthy. If an ex was using him for money (or, more likely, he was simply convinced that she was), make sure he knows that you're just the opposite.

- When he's relaxed with you, you can give him a massage or touch him in any way—he'll get the hint. He's sensitive with touch as well. Just don't rush things. Make sure he's in love before you go to bed with him. If you don't, he'll lose respect for you and think that you do the same with everyone.

Sensual Taurus

Taurus loves all sensual things—including food! And he loves domestic prowess. Cook a wonderful dinner for Taurus man or Taurus woman and you'll get extra potential husband or wife brownie points.

A woman Taurus wants to know that she's truly loved before she'll hit the sack with a man. She can have flings but, as she gets older and gets to know herself better, she'll realize that this is not the best of all possible worlds. She'll want to wait and be romanced. And there's no one who knows how to seduce and romance like Taurus.

Matches with Taurus

Conventional astrological wisdom says that the lot of us are better off with those who share the same element we do or with those who feed our element (Earth with Water, for instance). This makes Taurus compatible with other Earth signs (Virgo and Capricorn) and with Water signs. Unfortunately, other Earth signs—unless they have some Air in their charts—can sometimes be too serious for Taurus, who needs a good laugh in order to let his guard down. And though Virgo is more critical of himself (and thin-skinned with others' criticisms), Taurus can sometimes take it the wrong way, too.

Quite often, Taureans are fatally attracted to Scorpios, their polar opposites. Although their elements, Earth and Water, should make them compatible, this tends to be a superficial connection. Instead, beneath the surface, they're probably at war with one other. But this just kicks up the chemistry. Taurus is also very attracted to Fire signs. This may work okay in a relationship with a Leo, but in the long run, Sagittarius and Aries may just be too big a bite to chew for more down-to-earth Taurus.

Taurus and Leo

A huge problem with Taurus and Leo together is that Leo likes to spend! Taurus, while generous, is very concerned with having a nest egg. Therefore, he'll woo someone with expensive dinners in the beginning, but he'll come to resent anyone who makes him spend too much in the end.

Air signs mesh well with Earth signs, too, because they're both thinking signs, whereas Water and Fire signs are more spontaneous and apt to follow their hearts more. Gemini will entertain Taurus, but Taurus won't necessarily trust her. Libra may be a good bet for Taurus, as both have an incredible affinity for an elegant, sumptuous, and refined life. Libra and Taurus manage to acquire it together by spurring each other on. Aquarius' lifestyle will drive conservative Taurus crazy, despite his attraction to her.

Virgo in Love

Virgos are inscrutable in the affairs of the heart. They seem remote and quiet one minute, then open and talkative the next. This is due only to Virgo's battle within himself. He's sensitive but doesn't like to show it. Sometimes he'll need to show you how he feels; other times, he'll keep his feelings a secret. Unfortunately, he doesn't always let you see this true side of himself. He's too busy weighing all the options and trying to act the way he thinks he should, not how he truly feels.

Virgos always need to perfect everything: every moment, every deed, and every word. They're idealists, but in a practical way. They believe that everything should fall into place on its own (even if it shows no sign of happening) and tend to stay in relationships much longer than they should simply because they don't want to give up and walk away. To them, you are the investment of their precious time. They also hold on to the past like Cancers and, unfortunately, apply past experiences to present ones. In a perfect world, this would make sense (to them). Unfortunately, each situation is different, and Virgos must face this fact.

It is said that Virgos generally don't entertain romantic illusions. There is truth to this, but it's not the whole story. Virgos are incredibly romantic when they feel it. They have a wonderful appreciation of love—and know how to woo the "right" way. They seem more practical than idealistic but deep down, Virgos suffer for love and feel their emotions intensely.

Virgos try to make everything fit into their idea of a perfect world. For example, they're very serious about the words they and others use. If you tell a Virgo something, he expects you to follow through on your promise. He's put his heart and soul into finding a solution for you. If you don't at least try it his way, he'll seriously discredit you.

Are Virgos Critical?

Yes. Don't take it personally, though. A Virgo is never harder on the people he loves than he is on himself. Virgo needs to analyze, sort through, and mentally take stock once in a while in order to feel grounded and stable.

Here's the bottom line: If you ask Virgo for advice, you'd better take it or at least make him think you're doing something practical about your situation. Like Sagittarius, Virgo will always tell you what to do and expect you to do it. If you get advice from Virgo and ignore it, he'll be less likely to help you in the future.

Seduction Tips with Virgo

Unfortunately, Virgos have a penchant for getting involved with emotionally abusive partners early on. Or it can go the other way: They have a relationship with someone they're able to boss around, but never quite get to the place where they respect a mate enough to stay with him or her in the long run.

Virgos, like Taurus, need to feel some kind of purity and sweetness in order to make love—even if he's not in love. He prefers being in love than not, and sometimes won't even have sex unless he's feeling love. One thing's for sure: Virgo must feel special, or it's just not happening. He can have adventurous affairs, but, as he gets to know himself, he'll simply want more and will despise the thought of getting close without the presence of deeper feelings.

- You have to do some grunt work to get on a Virgo's good side. If you show a Virgo that you're easy to get along with and can take his criticism with a healthy show of acceptance, he'll feel more comfortable with you and will eventually let his guard down completely.
- Virgos are conflicted within and, therefore, will come across as being nitpicky or too precise. The truth is, they've got thin skins. The best way to handle a Virgo lecturing and criticizing you is to tell her she's right about whatever she's picking at, at the moment. Then bring it up later to dispute, if you like. Virgos must have a sense that they're right. They know this about themselves.

Matches with Virgo

Virgos are mentally attracted to Geminis, but they find the twins a bit hard to take for the long run. The light, airy nature of Geminis, too, contrasts with Virgo's obstinate nature. Gemini likes interesting discussions (as does Virgo) and entertains Virgo well, but Virgo sometimes fights more than Gemini would like.

Instead, the "grounding" present in other Earth signs may seem appealing on the surface, but leave it to a Virgo to find fault with his fellow Earth signs. Scorpios and Cancers may be the best bets, with mystical Pisces a close second. Libra sometimes goes well with Gemini but it may seem like Virgo is always just round the bend with Libra—never quite getting all the love and devotion he wants. Libra makes it tough.

Fire signs can be great friends with Virgo, but the two might never truly understand the other's intentions, in general. It depends on the rest of their charts. If one is true Earth, and the other is true Fire, Virgo patronizes without knowing it, and sensitive Fire signs take offense without realizing that Virgo is just trying to help. In the end, anyone with a good heart and a sensitive but practical nature will get along well with Virgo, though. Like all astrological love matches, it all depends on the partners involved.

Capricorn in Love

At times, Capricorn needs a partner who is serious, while at other times he needs a lighthearted mate who will simply make him laugh. The latter will have an almost innocent quality—a purity—to which Capricorn is drawn. Which mate Capricorn ends up with, though, depends on where he is emotionally and mentally in life. This may be true for all of us to one extent or another, but it's especially true for Capricorn.

Ultimately, Capricorn's path is always serious business. No matter how hard you make him laugh about himself and the world, his path always leads back to the same riddle. Regardless of how hard he works, how far he climbs, or how emotionally or physically rich he becomes, it's never enough. It only leads back to solitude of self.

That said, Capricorns can be very independent. They don't like being told what to do or how to do it. They seem malleable enough, and can get along with anybody, though they don't necessarily enjoy the company of all. A mate must be stimulating, engaging, knowledgeable, and, most importantly, grounded, in order for Capricorn to respect her.

If Capricorn senses that his partner is off kilter, he'll run for the hills. He won't try to change her or help her as, say, Cancer would.

Meanwhile, if you're getting words of passion, love, and forever after, pay attention. Capricorn doesn't spew out or toss around romantic words just to woo you and then leave you cold. He's got to be somewhat convinced in order to do it. True, he's a little better at having meaningless adventures than Virgo is, but eventually he'll want something that means family and future to him. And he takes that very seriously, indeed.

Seduction Tips with Capricorn

Capricorn wants a loyal, stable, solid, and devoted partner. If you have a huge group of friends (like Aquarius) and don't give Capricorn his due, you can forget it. Capricorn needs to know that you'll be there when he needs you or he'll never consider you for the long term.

Financial Stability

Yes, Capricorn wants security with emotions but financial security is sometimes even more important. Not all Capricorns are great at earning money, but they're good at keeping it or saving it all for a rainy day. If you're a spender, and your Capricorn mate is not, watch out! This will drive Capricorn over the edge.

- Capricorns have a tough time walking away from a relationship, even one that's not that great. Therefore, you'll get little hints if Capricorn is not happy. They'll be subtle, though. If Capricorn, for instance, is spending a lot of time away from you or is talking more to others than to you—find out what's wrong before Capricorn pulls away completely. You'll always get some kind of tip-off.

- Capricorns can seriously appreciate sexiness but will admire a conservative style of dress even more. If you combine sexy with conservative, you've got it made. Actually, if you're able to dress for the occasion, Capricorn will adore this quality in you. Capricorn gets better at doing it himself, later in life, but he'll definitely notice if you make an effort for him.

Matches with Capricorn

Virgos may be too literal and spirited for Capricorn. Plus, Virgo in bed can bring out Capricorn's traditional side, which bothers Capricorn, who secretly longs for someone who can open him up, emotionally and spiritually (both in bed and out). Taurus may be too fixed, but because they both have the Earth element in common, Capricorn and Taurus can get along well.

Of all the Water signs, the intensity of Scorpios may be overwhelming—though Capricorn will get a real kick out of Scorpio's tendency to be jealous. In bed, these two can be smolderingly hot. Instead, the ambivalence of Pisces will, most likely, drive Capricorn nuts.

Capricorn and Cancer

Capricorns may just get along with Cancer because they're both Cardinal signs (though this could be a possible mad rush to the finish line, too! The two can be competitive!). Cancer and Capricorn both have refined senses of humor. If Capricorn has patience with Cancer's moods (not likely), this can work.

Strangely enough, a Leo might be the best bet for Capricorn. If Leo has some Earth in her chart—or some balanced Air—they get along well. Certainly, the attraction is there. Capricorn mystifies Leo. Capricorn praises Leo the way she needs to be praised. They complement each other, and that's what it's all about.

ASTROLOGICAL CHILDREN

Your Offspring and the Zodiac

Children are their Sun sign's purest form. However, the way we present ourselves to others is usually displayed by our ascendant—our rising sign. Your child will be a blend of the two, but his ascendant becomes more evident as he gets older. Read on to learn about your child's natural-born sign.

Your Aries Child

On a playground filled with children, an Aries child is easy to pick out. Most likely, he's organizing the others—telling them what to do, what they should play, what they should think, and directing the action. He's a natural born leader with smarts, talent, and tons of boasting power. And, if he's not this way yet, trust that he'll grow into it.

What he does isn't important; the thing is: He's always off doing something. He's very independent, too, so it wouldn't be surprising if he enjoyed a bit of time by himself. One thing's for sure, though: An Aries child knows how to get himself into trouble. He should be watched.

No Fear

An Aries child, just like the adult Aries, fears nothing. This is sure to send any overprotective parent into occasional fits. Watch your Aries child closely but still let him be himself. Too much criticism can stifle this born-to-be creative genius.

Creative and inspiring, an Aries child can be uplifting for any mother. However, when the child doesn't get her way, watch out for huge temper-tantrums. Even as adults, Aries tend to be big babies sometimes. But when an Aries child is feeling good, he's fun-loving, sweet, and tender. If your Aries child is nurtured—but not overly spoiled—your little one will turn out to be a romantic, chivalrous man or a sweet, charming woman.

Your Taurus Child

This child may be a loner or she may just prefer one or two friends to a group of buddies. When she plays, she has fixed ideas about how the play should proceed. In fact, just like the stubborn bull she is, she sometimes has problems with authority and a strange, idealistic view of the way things need to be done.

Taurus children are famous for their patience. This can work for you or against you. They'll never tire of wanting what they want. They're not likely to give up easily, even if their attachment is one that is completely unhealthy for them. They're idealists, and they suffer from "good girl" syndrome.

Encourage Taurus children to explore their own creativity: art, music, drama, or simply an appreciation of these things. They benefit from the rhythms of nature, from being outside and also by engaging in physical activity. When a Taurus child gets tense, it shows up in the neck area. Therefore, she benefits greatly from massage and physical exercise.

Your Gemini Child

As toddlers, Gemini children are impatient. They don't bother learning to crawl—they're trying to walk as soon as their legs are strong enough to support them. Once they learn to communicate, they challenge you at every step with questions. They must know the reason for everything.

Gemini children are fascinated by the mundane; they can find humor in the ridiculous. They also have an affinity for the overdramatic. Gemini children are born actors.

These kids are precocious but inconsistent in the way they express it. Some days a Gemini will lead the neighborhood kids into anarchy; the next day he or she might keep company with a book, microscope, or pet. They like the furry warmth and security of a dog or a cat and enjoy observing how animals live on a daily basis. Just watch out: They may be studying people or pets in order to put the odds in their favor!

Don't try to pigeonhole your Gemini child. Instead, accept this fact and try to provide a learning environment in which your Gemini can explore who she is. Be prepared for a wild ride but feel good about knowing that your Gemini child is a versatile, incredibly impressive little person!

Your Cancer Child

The Cancerian youngster marches to the beat of a different drummer. Don't expect detailed explanations about how your Cancerian is feeling. If she's in the mood, she might tell you how so-and-so hurt her feelings today at school. But if she's not in the mood, nothing you can say will prod her to explain.

This child is often dreamy. She would rather read a book than run around outside, unless the activity or sport happens to interest her. In a group, she's likely to take the easy way out and go along with the crowd. Or she may remain completely passive about the situation.

Cancer children usually pick one of their parents as the favorite. In fact, they can get overly possessive with one or the other. The best way to remedy this is to not cater to the child's need for the one—make sure that your child gets equal time with both parents. At worst—this child is moody. At best, though, she's incredibly sweet.

Dealing with a Cancer Child

The Cancerian child needs to feel that he is an integral part of the family unit and is appreciated. As a child, he needs to nurture and be nurtured. Therefore, as a parent, your best route to communication with a Cancer child is acceptance and gentle guidance.

Your Leo Child

As toddlers, little Leos keep you running. Their abundant energy fuels them from sunrise to midnight, and by the time you fall into bed, you're ragged. As they mature, Leo kids are surrounded by other children, so your house is likely to be the gathering place for your Leo's youthful tribe. Leos are bossy, but your Leo child is sensitive, too, and this can sometimes be a problem in terms of communication.

Leos have big hearts. Leo children instinctively understand which other children are similar to them, yet they don't care. They'll make friends with anyone who is "a good person," in their eyes. This has a negative side: They can be easily influenced by the wrong crowd.

The innate generosity of this sign manifests itself early. Leo kids feel compassion toward people less fortunate than they are. They're likely to bring home strays of all shapes and sizes. They also tend to be fearless, accept every dare, and take risks that will turn you gray before your time.

Your Virgo Child

You'd better know how to think quickly when you're around a Virgo child. They're impatient, and they possess boundless energy. They love to learn, and their curiosity prompts them to poke around in everything. When they feel passionate about something, they bring the full power of their entire being to that particular endeavor.

This child is inclined to fluctuating moods, the cause of which originates in the mind rather than in the emotions. If they can't understand something, their frustration mounts until they either explode or work to finally understand the problem. The compassion that marks them at a young age usually deepens with time. They also love animals.

Virgo children do tend to be a bit cleaner than other children. Even as babies, they have a sense of personal space and, more than likely, would rather their room be clean and tidy, than messy and cluttered.

They also love music, dancing, and even conversation with strangers once they warm up. Human interaction is more essential to their development than watching television or a video. Meanwhile, you'll be amazed at what a genius your Virgo baby is!

Your Libra Child

Chances are good that you won't find a Libra baby or child rolling around in a sandbox or looking for bugs. Their sensibilities are usually too refined for that. The typical Libra child is more likely to be reading a book or listening to music.

Libra children enjoy group activities and get along well with others kids in a group. They usually have one special friend with whom they confide. Don't be alarmed, though, if your Libra toddler has an imaginary friend that she talks about and plays with. This is common with Libra babies.

Talk, Don't Shout

Never shout at a Libra child. She's extremely sensitive. She will cower, concede, and then resent you for it. Instead, just tell her what behavior you object to and extract a promise that the problem won't be repeated.

Libra children are well known for their sense of fair play. Though they love to be in the spotlight—an only child especially—they're quickly brought around to a sense of right and wrong if they're taught this at a young age. They learn how to share long before other children do.

Many Libra children may start trouble and then take off before the going gets rough. At this point, though, their curiosity is unimaginably high, and they'll go off to a safe spot and watch the chaos unfold at a distance. Libra children have a good sense of character and are people watchers.

Your Scorpio Child

From infancy, these children are usually distinctive in some way. They form their opinions early, based on what they experience and observe. Their intensity and depth of emotions is legendary, even at an early age. They can have outbursts of temper when they don't get their way or terrible bouts of crying when their feelings are hurt.

Scorpio children can be manipulative. They're sometimes sneaky and incredibly secretive. It's tough to know which way they're going so you'll have to keep tabs on your Scorpio child. Unfortunately, they're so intense—even as children—that they can be prone to depression or self-pity. It's highly unlikely that your Scorpio child will be superficial on any level, even if he puts up a wall to others and appears to be so.

Check It Out

As the parent of a Scorpio child, there are times when you'll be completely puzzled over your child's behavior. Don't leave it alone. Investigate. Instead of trying to guess what's wrong, just be forthright and ask.

Scorpio children flourish in an environment that is rich with variety, but they need their own space. Scorpio kids are very bright. They may never get around to reading, but they'll be happy to know books are there for them.

Scorpio children are masters at human behavior and exhibit deep knowledge and wisdom long before you'd expect it. Scorpios are all about transformation. As a parent, a Scorpio child will change your outlook on life forever!

Your Sagittarius Child

From the time he is old enough to have friends, the phone will never stop ringing for your Sagittarius child. These kids possess such optimism and vivacity that other kids are drawn to them. Sagittarius children are always the center of attention. They're wise and helpful—even if they have a serious problem with authority.

A Sagittarius child's candor may be welcome with friends but it may not sit well with you or with other adults. Both Sagittarius children and adults have a refined sense of sarcasm and wit and call it as they see it—even if it hurts someone's feelings. They're direct but generally lack tact.

On the other hand, a Sagittarius child may refuse to surrender his opinion to anyone. Sagittarius children make decisions on who is "worthy" of their attention. If another child or adult has lost a Sagittarius child's respect, this child won't give him the time of day. Yet Sagittarius kids are also warm, loving, and generous with those they deem important.

As a parent of a Sagittarian child, your best approach is to establish the parameters of authority early. Always allow your child the freedom to say what she thinks and believes, even if you don't agree. The Sagittarian child needs to know she won't be reprimanded for standing up for what she believes.

Your Capricorn Child

Capricorn children can converse as easily with other kids as they can with adults. They seem wise beyond their years. In fact, they're sometimes more at ease with adults. In some respects, Capricorn children actually regard the adults in their lives as equals. However, this doesn't mean that they never act like kids. When they loosen up, they can be wild and unpredictable; silly and goofy. But they're probably almost never reckless.

The Need for Limits

Capricorn children need boundaries. They feel safer and more secure with a schedule and a plan. If they're allowed to do anything they want at any time, they will feel uncomfortable. Give them chores they'll enjoy every once in a while.

Like their adult counterparts, Capricorn children attack whatever they do with efficiency and patience. They often exhibit deep compassion for less fortunate people. As the parent of a Capricorn child, you may even have to teach him to lighten up! But, also, you'll relate well with your wonderful Capricorn child.

Your Aquarius Child

Aquarius children don't recognize barriers of any kind among people, so their friends span the gamut of the social and economic spectrum. They tend to be extroverts, but can also be content in solitary pursuits. They can be as stubborn as Taurus children, particularly when it comes to defending something they believe in.

Aquarius, though outwardly gregarious, likes freedom and time spent alone. She tends to be a bad judge of character because she always finds the good in everyone. Even as a child, she plays with everyone and is a loyal friend. However, once someone has wronged her, she won't hesitate to cut this person out and eject him from the sandbox.

Even though these kids get along well with their peers, Aquarius children aren't afraid to disagree with the consensus. Within a family structure, they need to have the freedom to speak their own minds and know that their opinions will be heard. They may chafe at rules that are too rigid and strict—and they simply detest criticism. It cuts them to the core.

Remember, too, that Aquarius will take things in stride but that freedom with careful consideration works best. They have to know that you care but aren't on top of them all the time. Do this, and you'll have a generous, bright, and charming Aquarius child!

Your Pisces Child

In a crowd, the easiest way to pick out a Pisces child is by her smart, discerning eyes. Her gaze seems wise and almost ancient. Little Pisces girls sometimes come off as snobs to others who don't know them well; Pisces boys can come off as stuck-up or all knowing. These traits are innate. They simply have a certain inbred regality, like little princesses and princes.

It sometimes seems that a young Pisces is not listening to you; that's not the case. A Pisces child hears everything and will surprise you when she revives the subject at any given time. Even as a child, Pisces is caring and sweet. His mind is always working. He thinks too much and worries a lot, contributing to his idealism and desire to make the world a better place.

Dreamers

Pisces children tend to have vivid dreams. Many Pisces children also show an early interest in psychic phenomena. If the mystical tendencies are nurtured and encouraged, a Pisces child can grow into a true medium, psychologist, clairvoyant, and/or healer.

These children feel everything with such intensity that a cross look is probably all a parent needs to keep them in line. Their feelings are easily hurt. However, if other children challenge them, they will stand up for themselves.

Pisces children are paradoxes—equally strong and insecure. They long to find their own way and yet, once they do, they are sought out constantly by other children for pep-talks and good advice. Pisces is nurturing, sweet, and always knows what to say to everyone. Her sense of diplomacy is the stuff of legends—even with her parents. You'll feel lucky to have a Pisces child at your side!

ASTROLOGY AND HEALTH

Charting Your Well-Being

The part of astrological lore dealing with health is often called Medical Astrology. Astrologers cannot cure diseases, of course, but astrology can be extremely helpful in predicting when various parts of the body are most vulnerable to harm and the duration of the disease or condition.

See a Doctor

It should go without saying that if you find yourself suffering from illness or another medical condition or emergency, consult a physician at the earliest possible opportunity. Astrology is no substitute for a visit to the doctor.

Houses and Signs

Generally, medical issues are governed by the sixth house and its planetary ruler as well as the ascendant on your birth chart. Saturn affects chronic conditions, while Mars affects acute ones. In addition, you need to understand which parts of the body are ruled by which houses and signs.

First house or Aries: Head, face, brain, complexion

Second house or Taurus: Teeth, speech, right eye, throat, cerebellum, neck

Third house or Gemini: Right ear, shoulders, collar, hands, lungs

Fourth house or Cancer: End of life, chest, breast, ribs, stomach, digestive system

Fifth house or Leo: Heart, mind, spinal column

Sixth house or Virgo: Disease, kidneys, bowels, abdomen

Seventh house or Libra: Waist, navel, lumbar region, skin

Eighth house or Scorpio: Urinary system, sex organs, pelvic bones, anus

Ninth house or Sagittarius: Hips, arterial system, nervous system

Tenth house or Capricorn: Knees, hams, joints, bones

Eleventh house or Aquarius: Legs, ankles, left ear

Twelfth house or Pisces: Lymphatic system, feet and toes, left eye

Planets

In addition, as mentioned, the planets and the Sun and Moon have a significant effect on various parts of your body. These are:

Sun: Heart, eyes, blood circulation, spinal cord, right eye in males and left eye in females

Moon: Lung-related diseases, kidneys, stomach, uterus, sanity, left eye in males, right eye in females

Mercury: Digestive system, nervous system, lungs, speech-related issues, mouth, tongue, hands, epilepsy

Venus: Throat, neck, skin, reproductive organs, STDs

Mars: Forehead, nose, muscles, male reproductive organs, burns, cuts, fevers, accidents, electrical shock

Jupiter: Liver, diabetes, right ear, obesity

Saturn: Weakness, teeth, bones, knees, joints, chronic disease, asthma, skin

Uranus: Brain, spinal cord, heart attacks, sudden accidents

Neptune: Epilepsy, insanity, drug addiction, insomnia, infectious diseases

Pluto: Congenital diseases, diseases due to exposure to radiation

If you want to determine the way in which your chart can be interpreted concerning your health, think back to several times in the past when you were ill or suffered a physical injury. Draw up charts for those times and examine them to see how your ill health manifested itself in your horoscope.

Nicholas Culpeper (1616–1654)

Culpeper was widely hailed in his day as an herbalist and physician. He was also a noted astrologer, who regularly consulted his charts concerning his patients. So much so, apparently, that the Society of Apothecaries accused him of witchcraft, and he had to rein in his practices.

Herbal Remedies and Astrology

Various herbs used in remedies for diseases are ruled by the different houses. Here is a list of some of the most widely used natural sources of healing and their associated houses.

Aries: Garlic, mustard, cayenne, ginger, sassafras

Taurus: Violet, plantain, thyme, tansy, cowslip

Gemini: Parsley, dill, fennel, flax, caraway

Cancer: Meadowsweet, pumpkin, peppermint, chamomile

Leo: Rosemary, mistletoe, St. John's wort, bay laurel

Virgo: Anise, coriander, oregano

Libra: Thyme, cranberry, corn silk, barberry

Scorpio: Aloe, ginseng, wormwood, raspberry

Sagittarius: Dandelion, sage, lime blossom, maple syrup

Capricorn: Mullein, comfrey, horsetail, wintergreen

Aquarius: Lemon balm, lavender

Pisces: Poppy, echinacea, mugwort

ASTROLOGY AND FINANCE

Finding Money in the Planets

Astrology offers predictions, both general and specific about the future, so it's hardly surprising that astrologers are regularly consulted about money matters. This can take the form of predictions about movements within the stock market; it can also mean learning which signs are most propitious for saving and for making new, significant purchases.

Planets and Money

While Saturn is generally responsible for bringing in a regular income over time, Venus is strongly connected with your ability to save. That said, any planet can affect your personal finances as well as market trends depending on what sign is in the ascendant. Various planets are controllers of finances for the houses.

- Saturn controls the economies of Aries and Pisces
- Jupiter controls the economies of Taurus and Aquarius
- Venus controls the economies of Cancer and Sagittarius
- Mercury controls the economies of Leo and Scorpio
- Mars controls the economies of Gemini and Capricorn
- The Moon controls the economy of Virgo
- The Sun controls the economy of Libra

"Controls" in this case means "influences." The influence can be negative or positive.

Business Astrology

Astrology can also give insights into trade and business. Indian astrology (also sometimes referred to as Vedic astrology) places considerable emphasis on astrological influences in commerce and money. As with money, planets rule various houses, but the order is somewhat different.

- Aries trade and commerce are controlled by Venus and judged by Libra
- Taurus trade and commerce are controlled by Mars and judged by Scorpio
- Gemini trade and commerce are controlled by Jupiter and judged by Sagittarius
- Cancer trade and commerce are controlled by Saturn and judged by Capricorn
- Leo trade and commerce are controlled by Saturn and Uranus and judged by Aquarius
- Virgo trade and commerce are controlled by Jupiter and Neptune and judged by Pisces
- Libra trade and commerce are controlled by Mars and judged by Aries
- Scorpio trade and commerce are controlled by Venus and judged by Taurus
- Sagittarius trade and commerce are controlled by Mercury and judged by Gemini
- Capricorn trade and commerce are controlled by the Moon and judged by Cancer
- Aquarius trade and commerce are controlled by the Sun and judged by Leo
- Pisces trade and commerce are controlled by Mercury and judged by Virgo

INDEX